GLOBAL CITIZEN

"I admire the way Stan Chung uses his own self-questioning
narrator to ground and personalize the situations, issues and
observations he tackles. A refreshing, inclusive honesty surfaces
in this collection of essays. When combined with the gift
he has for capturing the detail and texture of the lives we all
inhabit, the result is writing that matters because it
both includes and illuminates."

JOHN LENT, AUTHOR

"I read every column Stan Chung writes with fascination.
He has a rare capacity for exploring his own psyche in a way that
connects with mine and, I suspect, with most of us.
Always, I am moved – sometimes to laughter, sometimes to
a wry grin of recognition, sometimes to tears."

JIM TAYLOR, COLUMNIST, CO-FOUNDER OF WOOD LAKE BOOKS
AND AUTHOR OF 17 BOOKS

"Stan Chung's essays speak of the details, dreams, desires, and
occasional dead ends that map the larger, global experience of the
Canadian Everyman/woman. The writing is superb.
Chung writes from the heart, the gut, the knees, and generously
contributes to the genre of creative non-fiction with a localized,
vernacular flair that speaks honestly to the experience of a "global
citizen" in small town Canada. In the end, Chung connects the
dots between local and global experience through the story-telling
itself, through the shared experience of the conflicted, flawed,
love-able, and always real human condition. Good stories,
good writing, and, a very good read."

VERONICA GAYLIE, AUTHOR OF THE LEARNING GARDEN.

My parents, Ji Won Chung and Sook Ja Chung.
June 1961, Seoul, Korea

STAN CHUNG

GLOBAL CITIZEN

RIVER OF LOVE & OTHER ESSAYS

TEAM PUBLISHED WITH ARTISTIC WARRIOR PUBLISHING

Ordering Information: Quantity sales. Special discounts are
available on quantity purchases by corporations, associations,
and others. For details, contact the author at:
stanchung@gmail.com.

Global Citizen:
River of Love & Other Essays
Stan Chung
ISBN: 978-1-987982-22-0 (pbk), 978-1-987982-23-7 (eBook)
Fourth Printing

Team published with
Artistic Warrior Publishing
www.artisticwarrior.com

Table of Contents

STAN CHUNG

Introduction

"Let everyone sweep in front of his own door,
and the whole world will be clean." — GOETHE

GLOBAL CITIZEN came to fruition as a newspaper column in October of 2006. I chose the title because global citizenship is a seductive yet contradictory term. Some prefer the concept because it recognizes the transnational character of our problems. If our problems cross national boundaries, then surely solutions require a mobilization beyond national scope.

However, this transnational view of the world is problematic for the average citizen. While we know that many economic, social, and environmental issues require collaborative solutions, it remains difficult for thoughtful people to know what to do. Should we look to keep our own doorways swept clean as Goethe suggests, or go across the ocean and get busy on someone else's doorway?

Some in the developing world ask us to mind our own damn business; others beg for our assistance. Do we support the local producer and keep our own employed, or do we support developing countries in order to decrease the gap between the rich and poor?

The average woman dies at the age of 34 in Somalia. What can I possibly do about that?

Should we, through our collective purchasing power, make the rich countries poorer and the poor countries richer? Will a Somali woman's lifespan be extended by this strategy? And if we believe this is the right thing, what will we do when our economic autonomy, even our own sovereignty, becomes threatened by transnational power? Isn't this what makes globalization such a problematic term?

What do we have to give up so that hospitals can be built in Somalia? How will giving aid to Somalia improve the fate of women? How do my personal choices make a difference while still respecting human agency?

These questions torture us in their superficial simplicity. To be a global citizen may sound like a good thing, but how exactly does one choose to behave? How do you make a difference to people who are uneducated, malnourished, victimized by patriarchy and colonialization, made destitute by desertification, without becoming seduced by our own colonizing tendencies?

Will our actions make a difference? Or is the concept of individual action just another way in which true power and authority divert us from the truth?

Closer to home, we try to support our local farmers. If we can, we ride our bikes to work. We hurriedly buy compact fluorescent bulbs while barely realizing the extent of our actions. Our citizenship has been equated more with consumer expenditure and less with protest and critical thinking. Consumer as global citizen turns out to be not only a bit of a contradictory term, but a great deception.

In whose interest is it that our freedom is now equated with the freedom to purchase? Our identities are defined by what we buy. We are defined by our cars, houses, and music. Rebellion, activism, critical thinking — these things are now associated with brands and products that make us feel as if we are independent individuals brimming with autonomy and free choice.

Just give me my coffee and yoga pants.

Do our tattoos, mopeds, and vegan meals mean anything other than the fact that we think we are what we purchase? No matter what we choose, how trendy/state of the art/enlightened — no matter how we reflect the illusion of our freedom, no matter if our choices are union made or child slave made, somebody has convinced us that our individual inaction is to blame.

Materialism has become our cage. We seem to know of no other way to express citizenship other than to employ our purchasing power. And who controls what we purchase? Who makes us believe we can buy our way out of environmental disaster? Who makes us desire products as freedom? Who makes us think we are autonomous individuals?

The combined forces of education, media, government, and corporation — they all want us to keep dreaming and purchasing. Whether it's the MBA to buy the BMW or the arms company that allows soldiers to buy Tim Hortons donuts in Afghanistan, we also seem to think our happy lifestyles are worth exporting.

What happens should we wake up from this dream? What happens when we realize that our rich and comfortable lives are not driven by us, but by forces that will not allow us to stop?

What do we do then? Where is our human freedom?

With our minds controlled by media corporations and advertisers, the odds seem against us. To ride our bikes, grow our vegetables, and watch PBS — these things seem like wholly insignificant defences.

Yet, human beings are a rebellious lot. What do we do? How do we stop? How do we slow it down? How do we wake up?

So the term global citizen is an ironic title for a newspaper column and a book. I especially have no credentials. In fact, if I am being honest, my lifestyle is a model for 21st century hypocrisy.

Hypocrisy. Paralysis. Privilege. That's me on a good day.

Now that last line is a piece of middle-class self-loathing that only the truly privileged could utter. After all, you could see me as a poster boy of success. I was born in another country, came to Canada without knowing a lick of English, and today, I own property, work as a leader in academia, speak and write English with the authority of a native, and have a strong sense of community to boot.

I also possess an unbelievably wicked sense of first world entitlement. I demand fast, good, and cheap. I demand everything to be a win-win. I demand that we stop global warming and make some damn good money while we do it. I demand that we develop the downtown, house the homeless, and make the poor invisible.

I want it all. I want it now.

I want a Porsche, extra wide bike lanes, and zero development after I am done buying up property.

People like Bono and other celebrities working for good causes make us think we are moving forward at least in consciousness. But we all know that jet-setting for the globe takes a lot of jet fuel. We all know that for every two steps forward, we could easily be taking three steps back. You want me to consume less? You want to me have less than my neighbours? You want me to give stuff up?

Screw you.

What is my puny individual sacrifice going to do exactly? Assuage my middle-class guilt? Help the baby boomers feel less excited about their equity and big fat pensions? And on top of all this, I'm supposed to feel good about the incremental changes that we, after great deliberation, finally agree upon?

Incremental change won't do it. We all know that driving a hybrid and eating organic are not really revolutionary acts.

What will dutifully recycling my garbage, investing in ethical mutual funds, and spending travel funds on "volunt-tourism" projects mean compared to the emissions produced by industrial China and India?

We all know people who say, "Why should anybody give up anything? This is my nightmare and I paid for it."

I need my three televisions and six computers. I need wireless Internet and stainless steel appliances. My family is a corporation, and I need to maximize shareholder value. I demand to sprinkle on odd *and* even days, damn it!

Before I turn you off reading this book, I want to say that there is nothing like writing a column to help you broadcast your own hypocrisy. After this phase of thinking, I started wanting to better understand why I was such a hypocrite. So I thought about my parents, my upbringing, my education, and my ancestors.

That move brought the column increased attention.

I never thought anybody would care to hear about my parents, their struggles, and my upbringing as the son of a Korean-born United

Church minister. I never thought my experience extraordinary. I never thought it atypical, nor did I find it very interesting. Everybody has a story; my story begins and ends just like everyone else's.

So I took the column into personal experience without much reflection as to where I was headed. In then end I found myself searching for my father. I will always be searching for him. My father is an immense influence upon me. He is my saviour and my captor. He sets me free; he cages me. My resistance to his influence is futile.

I detested and became him.

I tell you, being a global citizen is not an easy form of hypocrisy. It begins with the kind of critical consciousness where you not only challenge how you do business, how you choose the things you choose, but it finally ends up with you questioning who the hell you really are.

As I explored my parents, childhood, and my own family, I did not know what I was writing. What was this form that I was writing which was part essay, part confession, part memoir? Whatever it was, readers in ways that continually surprised me greeted these explorations enthusiastically.

Every time I submitted something to the editor that filled me with dread and anxiety, readers rewarded me with emails telling me things that I cannot repeat here without sounding like a combination Deepak Chopra, David Sedaris, and Stuart McLean.

These emails came in bunches whenever I wrote something that struck an emotional chord with readers. Readers told me they cried.

The column began to change as I tried to push the emotional content of the work, to take bigger risks, to talk openly about the suicide of a student, the death of my mother, how my parents abandoned me. People tolerated the experimentation. They tolerated the kind of disclosure that makes most very nervous or at least nauseous.

You made me feel like the risk was worth it.

I was always taught to take risks in my writing. The more I risked, the more I realized that the column was becoming an intensely personal way of connecting with my community. I didn't care about being a columnist of a national newspaper. I cared when local people came up to me on the street, shook my hand, slapped me on the back, and told me to keep it up.

Today, with the publication of this book, all my romantic notions about what community means and what community can do for you in a reciprocal relationship have been realized. It is a tremendous feeling to hear that you have either made a difference in someone's life or been the catalyst for some personal reflection.

Even though I have been practicing writing since the age of eight, my writing self-esteem wavers. I keep writing because I want to understand; I keep writing because I want to keep improving.

These essays and stories are united by a passion for writing. Writing is a key part of my identity; I write because this is one of the ways I learn best. I don't know something until I spell it out. You could say I don't know what I think or feel without trying to write it down in less than 1200 words to an audience of 30,000 Okanagan citizens.

I do want to write something down now. I want to say thank you. Thank you for helping me discover myself and become a small part of your lives. You are a big part of mine.

Man of Winter

Early morning, white sheet covering the world, the seasons roll on. But for me it is the shoulder, the space between seasons that makes me lie in bed desperately trying to remember the dream I had about my father, the one where he is talking to me, and I'm listening. And he is so real.

"I want to tell you something," my father says in these dreams that feel like missed episodes of old television shows.

Inside the dream, we speak an unknown language. I remember fragments when I awake, the light pooling on the ceiling, the rhythm of the morning sounding through the house. Where are you father? My father comes to me. In winter.

As a boy he dived for abalone on the island of Cheju, a tropical oasis between Korea and Japan. Cheju is centred by a dormant volcano. Things grow well there. Lush. The boy runs without shoes. He delights in fishing, in fighting other boys with flying kites, crushed glass glued to kite string, and he dreams, too. Does he dream of me? Does he dream of the son that will grow up in a cold country far away from the comfort of his native tongue, far away from salted grilled fish that his mother grills over fruit wood?

He is a man of winter. His coolness astounds me. In dreams we speak on busses. We are in Seoul in the morning, dressed in office suits. "A man keeps his word," he begins and then the dialogue fades. My father, I realize, is giving me more than advice now. He is telling about the nature of coldness, about human separation, about the temperature of families.

Oh, this coolness — why does he tell me he loves me only after he is gone? Oh, this coolness. I know he loves me by the way he lets me forget him. He is December, chickadees on the line, pine boughs under weight, your future blanketed with white. In winter, things are different. No green shots, twirling leaves, or high noon. In winter things are different. My father arrived in Canada in 1965, a man without good English or a good coat, studying theology at UBC.In a bent photograph, the surprise of snow registers in his eyes. Snow covers the curves of cars, blankets arbutus trees, and accentuates his loneliness. What was he doing in this strange country, studying German, Greek, and Latin? Sorting out Tillich, Marx, and the word he whispers to me still — phenomenology. God, he says, feels like doubt. Doubt feels like being. Chew your food. Love sorrow. Feel the wind bend your body.

His impatience and ambivalence remain with me. He is a wanderer, never staying anywhere for long. Always living in the shoulder season, planning his next transition.Did he die a little bit every Canadian winter? Even though he was drawn to wilderness, drawn to the hardness of life as a voyageur. Even though he was drawn to brown down jackets, vast snow drifts in Maryfield, auger breaking through ice in Lac La Hache — kokanee and kim chee — he still found in winter a kind of paralysis, a slowing of the heart.Ten years ago, I was teaching English to forestry students up north. It was a dark afternoon, the colour of pulp smoke. We might have talked about punctuation, but instead we shared stories. One of the students, a bespectacled young man in a loose flannel shirt and unlaced boots told of his trap line.

"Sometimes though," he said quietly, "sometimes the trap doesn't kill the beaver. What do you do then?"

"I don't know if I want to say," he said."Please," we said.

"You don't want to waste a bullet. You don't want to ruin the pelt. So you hold the wounded animal in your arms," he said. "You put your hand over its heart. You press down. It takes awhile but soon it stops beating."

We know, the whole class knows, that this young man knows something about life that we rarely talk about. That this young man has shared something cold and true with us. Hunter and hunted are one. Human and animal are one. Life and death are one. Past and future are one. Father and son are ...

In Maryfield my father tried curling once. The curling boots became home to a family of mice. He never skied. He never played sports. He never came to the ice rink to watch me play hockey. He never went for long walks with my mother. He wanted to hunt though. And I followed him around, carrying a 12 gauge, wearing an impossibly orange vest, picking up animals by the leg. I delighted in winter as a boy. Doing angels. Making forts. Sliding in the night under the stars. Lying under falling snowflakes aiming my tongue at the dark sky. Wondering while lying in the snow what it might be to fall asleep, what it might be to remember these feelings, hang onto them so tight that future generations would remember me remembering. My son and daughter shoveled our long driveway this week. Did they remember me? During the winter, my father would sit downstairs in his study. He read serious books, novels by Updike, commentaries on the Bible, the *Observer* magazine (edited by Jim Taylor), *Christian Century*, and a small magazine called *Upper Room*. This magazine helped ministers come up with sermon ideas.

He sat in his office six days a week, my father, perfecting his sermon, warming his feet on the electric heater, a brown cardigan with leather buttons and suede patches covering his shoulders, and at about four o'clock in the afternoon he would pad upstairs, his brow wrinkled still lost in thought and sit in the living room looking out at the street. I didn't know at that time that he was thinking about me and my sister, how we were faring in school, what we wanted for Christmas, and what kind of people we would become. I am sure of this now.

In our strange dream language we are laughing about our parallel lives. You knew that? Yeah, dad. Really? He tells me things that I do not understand yet, but I know by his bright eyes and quiet voice that the time of understanding will come. This understanding will come mostly in the heart of winter. When the world is cold. And dark and still.

Catch and Release

"To every thing there is a season, and a time to every purpose under the heaven: A time to be born, and a time to die; a time to plant, and a time to pluck up that which is planted."
— ECCLESIASTES

She bit her lip with concentration. My nine-year-old girl balanced in the canoe. Her black hair moved in the breeze and settled on the collar of her life jacket. She held a fishing rod that bent at the tip as I paddled.

In the distance, spires of black spruce stood against the waist of the sky. Now that it was finally July, the sun had regained its heat.

Coolness rose off the water. I felt we were moving through the universe as one, even though the universe is just this small lake above Peachland, surrounded by craggy trees. It's summer again, I said to myself. She was nine years old, and this day was to surround and pass us as surely as the water swirled around the blade of the paddle.

In September on a bright Sunday, I held her small hand as we explored the spawning channels at Mission Creek Regional Park. The parking lot is crowded; there are exhibits to explore.

We entered the log museum and learned about the life cycle of the land-locked sockeye known as kokanee. We walked and talked about how this delicate and threatened creature fits so perfectly into the cycle of life, not just its own cycle from egg, alevin, and fry, to smolt and fingerling, but how the kokanee spawn, die, and are consumed by animals or returned to the soil as nutrients for other forms of life.

"These kids," my wife said to me that day, "they know more than we think."

The next night at dinner, we each took turns discussing our Monday.

"Did you ask any questions today?" I asked. We still find it very amusing that both our children like to raise their hands at the dinner table.

"Yes, Clementine?" I said with a mouthful of stroganoff. "You can put your hand down now."

"I asked her a question, and Daddy, I bet you can't guess what she said to me."

"I don't know. What did your teacher say?" I asked.

"Well, we talked about kokanee today and my teacher said she didn't even know the answer to my question!"

"Really? So what did you ask your teacher?"

"I asked her why the kokanee die after they lay their eggs. So, why do they die?"

"Well, honey, hmm, gee, that's an excellent question," I said wondering what to say next.

"I guess nobody knows the answer to that one," said my wife.

I glanced at Clementine. We named her after the delicately-skinned orange that her mother craved when she was pregnant. Clementine's brown eyes nearly exploded with curiosity at the thought of her question.

Why did the kokanee die? I had no explanation. Why did this small fish, that struggled so heroically against the odds in order to return to its origins and lay its eggs, conclude its journey with — with death?

I remembered a few years back walking along Deep Creek at Hardy Falls Regional Park near Peachland. The red carcasses of exhausted worn out fish were strewn everywhere along the creek, the smell of rotting flesh inescapable. It looked like a massacre. I couldn't stand the sight or the stench or the true meaning of it all, and I ending up running down the path to escape. Daddy is just exercising, I told the kids.

After dinner and a bath, I kissed her cheek and held my lips against her soft skin. "Good night, little girl. You're the best little girl in the world."

"And you're the best daddy in the whole wide world. You have a good sleep, too. I love you."

I wished for a moment that I could stop her from growing up, that I could with the force of my puny human will freeze her just as she appeared before me, a beautiful little girl poised at the beginning of an awakening. I wanted to keep her from growing up, protect her from losing the miraculous sense of wonder we can feel especially at this time of year.

Last weekend, we did as we always do at this time of year. We drove to our favourite farm on the Rutland bench. We stumbled out of the van, as eager as any family could be. It was time to pick grapes. Big, fat, luscious grapes. Grown under the hot summer sun.

We ducked under the vines, as we always do, and stood beneath them. It was so quiet under there. Black globes hung above us in huge pendulous clusters. Tight triangular spheres, dusky and filled with heavenly juice. The light beneath a grape vine, if you have not experienced it, is simply miraculous. I have never been to the great cathedrals of Europe, nor stood before the paintings of the Renaissance masters, but I imagine that the light could be no more holy, no more profound than the light filtering through an Okanagan grape vine.

My daughter gripped her bag of grapes and ran through the vineyard. This girl, she runs for no reason. She loves life. This girl twitches when she is standing still. She vibrates with energy. She leaps out of bed in the morning and tumbles into bed at night with glee. Without her, we would not live in quite the same way, not in the special way she teaches us.

When Clemo was a baby, I spent hours trying to rock her to sleep. My legs would cramp, my shoulders would sag, and I would think, like all fathers before and after me, that there was nothing more precious, no honour more glorious, than the privilege of being her father.

The fall reminds of us good things, and the quiet routine of life. Things ripen. Things are harvested. The peaches were good this year, weren't they? The cherries were elusive and sweet, like living chocolate. We loved our trips to buy fruit and pick fruit at local orchards. We found a farm in Armstrong last spring with tender asparagus. Those asparagus sweetened our hearts as did the plump bright tomatoes fattening in the hot corner of our yard.

There is a wild sensuality in eating with the seasons. Especially in this region where the bounty of local farms and our own gardens remind us that we are people of the earth, people who know deep in our genetic code that we are connected to nature. We know that we are nurtured and educated by the richness of the soil, the clarity of the water, and the passing of the seasons.

This season I will marvel at my little girl running through orchards. I will remember her telling us the story of the kokanee. I will watch her this year, as I did last year, and the year before, as she piles up the yellow leaves that have fallen from the sky. She will pile them up and jump in.

She will do it again and again. She will laugh with her brother. We will wave from the window. And we will try not to cry.

This time of year can make our ancient instincts come alive. These instincts arise despite the fact that we live comfortable and modern lives. A hundred years ago, before modernity, and maybe even centuries before when all we had were campfires, your kin and perhaps my kin would tend to their plants and await harvest.

Perhaps a long time ago, a long lost ancestor of yours or mine, would walk along a creek much like the one we call Mission Creek and wonder about the red fish. They would wonder, as we wonder now, why these fish spawn and then give up their lives. Yes, so that life can go on and on. So that our daughters will grow and show us that we will live on, too, even after the fall.

Letting Go

*"Whatever you are doing and wherever you are,
you will find steadiness, calm, and concentration if you
become conscious of your breathing."*
— MAJJHIMA NIKAYA

You thrash your arms and legs. Gasp for breath. The sky turns above you. You are drowning. Your heart smashes against sorrow, loneli-ness, and responsibility. You cannot breathe. Living is just like swim-ming, like when you were a boy with your father standing on the dock, watching you sputter and struggle and nearly die.

You are ten years old. You are twenty-six. You are forty-six. You are seventy-six. You know all about drowning.

The boy says you will learn to swim. Not just because your little sister is on the verge of doing it before you. You try not to resent the natural talents of others. You will learn to swim. And not just because you have been afraid of water your whole life, including nearly drowning twice, once on a swirling river when you were five and the other time in Pusan when you were two. The wave soared right over your head.

You like to think you remember — how you looked up at the wave at its crest, how you saw the underbelly of the wave, the grey blue water, starfish, dolphin, abalone, and receipts, so much smudged paper — the contents of your entire life — a clothesline of things all frozen above you — then the wave crashes and you awake, drowning.

Why is living like drowning?
At twenty-six, you blink yourself awake and tell yourself that you will finally become an adult, your self-sufficiency a goggle and mask that separates you from that boy you will always be.

At seventy-six you hear the television crackle in the living room. Dying frightens you, but you will learn how to swim because then your father will be proud of you. You have heroically refused help and so now you lay with a tube in your nose watching Rorschach shadows on the ceiling. What is scary is the feeling of your entire face being underwater. It overwhelms you. You don't like water up your nose. Your eyes fill up. You want to choke and spit. You don't want mouth-to-mouth resuscitation. You don't want to be helpless. What is also scary is your father's solemn face. He smiles only to himself. You used to play with his war medals and combat helmet. He has a scar on his neck from a stray bullet.

You are a boy. Other kids swim like rainbow trout. You learn slowly. Riding a bike came with scars. A skate cut your forehead when you were six. You worry about skating backward. Seven stitches in grade one. The bright lights of the Saskatchewan operating table. You may just drown again and again, like in your nightmares. So many things you cannot do.

It's late. You can't sleep. You feel hot. You think about whimpering. You do. You can't help it. Your mother still comes to your bed at night. Sometimes even your father. He sits reluctantly on your bed looking at the moonlight through the elm tree. Your bad dreams are not your fault – he wants to tell you. You dream about wandering the streets of Seoul where you are lost. You dream about Williams Lake where you are rolling endlessly off the knoll at city hall and onto Oliver Street traffic. At night the loneliness can be unbearable. So you whimper until one of them comes.

When are you going to stop whimpering? When will you? You don't know. You turn your pillow to the cool side. You are going to the lake tomorrow. You'll fish, you'll canoe, and maybe you'll think about swimming.

* * *

The sun sits high and yellow. You stand in the blue water up to your knees, now up to your thighs, now to your chest. Slipping into Chimney Lake makes you shiver. The muddy bottom sucks your feet. Mosquitoes dive. Flies buzz your ears. Slender weeds encircle your ankles like black eels.

You sit in the water and think. You put your face in after half an hour. You force open your eyes. You see mushroom-coloured ankles. You go to the shallows and stretch out your body. You hold your face in the water. You are a log now or a submarine or a boy playing dead. You put your face in again. Open your eyes again. You walk along the water with your hands on golden pebbles, like an alligator, like a boy who is summoning up the courage to float.

Suddenly you choke. You're drowning again. The sky spins. Your mother feels so far away. You see yourself in the future. A middle-aged man whispers to you — sometimes living is like drowning.

Floating is the greatest discovery of your life, you decide, when you are as you are now, poised on the precipice of darkness. Floating is part letting go, the boy tells you, and part trusting something else, the water, the push-back of God, the way the mattress bounces as your father sits on the edge of your bed and strokes your hair and tells you that you are a very good boy.

You are here, you say, as you float, balanced between letting go and hanging on. You trust that he knows that you will be okay, that he is always there, watching you, floating and sinking, floating and sinking ... you didn't know that swimming was the rhythm of life, rising and falling, living and dying, smiling and crying, to and fro, like the music you hear when you are finally underwater, the shifting shape of your father on the dock above you, smiling while you float.

***

And, yes, the boy is finally swimming now, kicking his legs, dipping his face in and opening your eyes to the truth of letting go. It is September now, a few months after Chimney Lake, and now you're doing the breast stroke for your father at Scout Island. He walks beside you on the dock as you swim. It is a cold day, and you are not dying.

Watch me, Daddy, you say.

Yes, I see you.

I'm swimming.

Yes, you are.

Watch me.

Let me hear you breathe, Son.

You are swimming then and now and always. You know that swimming is surrendering, like letting go and knowing your parents have sailed on. See them? I am waving in the distance. Stan Chung is waving at Stan Chung. You are ten years old. You are twenty-six, forty-six, seventy-six, and you are still learning to let go. Those who love you will always love you. Let me hear you breathe. Keep breathing. Watch me, Daddy. Watch me.

Summertime

"Summertime, and the livin' is easy. Fish are jumpin'
And the cotton is high." — GERSHWIN

Just like you, I have my good days where there is laughter, intimacy and hard work. I have my bad days, too, where it seems I am surrounded by a lack of community, by declining civility and where hard work means little. Then there is summer. Summer is a different time in the Okanagan.Summertime makes us feel scattered inside. Our emotions become thinner. We disappear at work. We reappear at the beach, but we are not really there either.One afternoon last week, our family and another two families were sitting at the beach. We were eating our dinner on a blue plaid blanket. There were a few dogs on the beach even though the signs said no dogs. There were some young people around. We could hear them swearing. Eff this and eff that. A few boats sped around, towing tubes. A man sat smoking on his jet ski while talking to his friends. All this is quite typical. You've been there, done that.

We had brought a little dinner picnic with us. We drank lemonade. Chewed our skewered pork. My wife has picnics in her soul, and we are thankful for her attentions to us. We swam. I walked up to my chest, took a deep breath and dived in. The water was sweet and cool. In the distance, we could see the faint smoke of the Terrace Mountain fire, but we knew that unlike 2003, this fire wasn't racing toward town ready to swallow us all.

We remembered sitting at Raymer Beach one day that fiery summer. The day was like night. We could not see across the lake. We could see maybe thirty meters in front of us; the smoke was so thick. We left the water, packed up and headed for the mall. We looked up at the sky in the mall parking lot. Huge flakes of black ash floated down and swirled over our heads. There was a yellow quality to the eerie light. It's hard not to forget that day.

For many, the memories from the firestorm of 2003 are still a little too close, like a bad dream from childhood.

Perhaps memories of that summer have made us less able to enjoy this summer. Perhaps other things are making us ill-at-ease. Perhaps it is all the complaining we hear about the recession, new city logo, harmonized sales tax, health care layoffs, bridge repair, visitors who never leave, and whatever else there is to complain about. Or could it be something about else? Something is ailing us, I believe. Sure, our friends are all out of town. Summertime is not when you grow closer to your friends. It is a time when we seem to be voluntarily lonely, when we reach for intimacy, confiding in no one but ourselves.

We drank our lemonade and gazed toward the new district of West Kelowna. We used to live across the lake in Rose Valley where a fire blazed a week or so ago. We have friends in Glenrosa, another lucky escape. Nobody feels safe, but there isn't much we can do, except try not to think about the fact that these fires were started by people, not by the single lightning strike of 2003. Just as we slip back into the water, we notice something floating in the water coming toward us, drifting with the current around a little rocky bend.

At first, we think we are seeing birds, but it is not birds we see. We count them. The kids count them. The people next to us see them and count them, too. My wife takes a deep dive and starts swimming out to these blue metallic objects. Yes, they are beer cans.

The beer cans are collected by us. My wife grabs one and throws it toward me. The man on the jet ski picks up at least half a dozen. His son, a little toddler in a life jacket, swims out and grabs another. I carry a can to the beach. Maybe we've all done our good deed for the day. We don't say much while this happens. My wife mumbles thank you to one of the men. Another guy, a young man with his girlfriend, puts the cans into a plastic bag. We go about our evening now. We go about our moment in paradise.

I don't know how you can throw a dozen beer into Okanagan Lake. I don't know how drunk you have to be. Nor do I understand why cigarettes are tossed out the window or how campfires are started during fire bans. I don't know why people text when they drive or why people get so confrontational about small things. But something inside me wants to blame something, even the weather.

Okay. It's hot. We crash our cars when it's hot. We pull weapons on each other. We say things we shouldn't. When it's hot, the sirens wail. While our visitors glorify our clean beaches, manicured wineries, and cool waters, our hospitals receive ambulance loads of people damaged by violence, inattentiveness, and irritation. We clearly have issues with summertime.

The Okanagan is mainly a summer resort, and like any resort, there is a fine line between celebration that is joyous and that which is reckless. The law of diminishing returns tells us how precious the first drink, how poisonous the last. How easy it is to be thoughtless. How easy to forget that we must share this paradise or lose it.

We continue to head to the beach on a daily basis. We have our special places where the water is clear and the beaches clean. We love it in the Okanagan. Sometimes, we are grateful that others do, too. But sometimes, we shake our heads. Sometimes, we plug our ears. Sometimes, we long for September.

River of Love

Your mother teaches you one simple thing above all others: how to love. Your mother shows you love, and you go out and practice, stumbling, fumbling, at once embracing and rejecting the river of her love. You love her and respect her, but you also think you know where the river ends.

The love that my mother showed me was at once beautiful and flawed. Her love is my map. It tells me where to go and where not to go. The current is steady with faithfulness, serenity, purpose, and obedience. Beneath the surface lies silence, suffering, anger, and bitterness. She cannot leap the banks and find a different way.

I did not know any of these things in November 1994 when I brought my mother to the guest room above the garage in my suburban home in Prince George, British Columbia. In July I was married, and she came to the wedding yellow-faced, jaundiced. I ruined my honeymoon with distraction and worry. In September, she was finally diagnosed with pancreatic cancer. In October, her surgery was deemed a failure. In November, she was given a few weeks to live. Without hesitation, I brought her home.

We tended to her. We willed her to live. And she lived until June, a miraculous eight months. Together, we saw the seasons. We saw autumn leaves crumble, winter snows wash away, pussy willows pop, and we saw summer in full flight. I had her for the last eight months of her life. I cooked for her. I cleaned for her. I laughed with her, and I exercised with her. I lifted her in my arms and carried her to the toilet. I sang to her, injected her with morphine, and stroked her forehead. I served her as she had served me.

Then I had to let her go.

In the end, I mothered my own mother, and I resisted losing her, even though it might have been better for her if I would have let her go sooner. But I could not. I could not let her go. And, in some ways, I still cannot.

Why? Because I know the truth about the entire experience of my mother's cancer, my care for her, and her death. Some called us noble. Some wondered how we survived the ordeal. Some asked how we did it. How did she live so long? How did she manage to walk until the very end when so many die in bed, only a shadow of their former selves? How did she manage to smile and care for others, as if she were supernatural?

I know the secret.

I know how she was able to pull it off. I even know how I was able to do the things that I cannot believe I did. I know how it happened. I know how I got the strength and devotion. I know how she got the power. Yes, I know the secret. At every single moment of our eight months together, this frail Korean woman of 52, overtaken by a violent and fast-growing cancer, consumed with intense pain and agony, and still suffering from the loss of her husband to schizophrenia, was still mothering me.

I was her son. And she helped me through the whole thing. I was not mothering her. *She* was mothering me.

As I watched her die, as I watched her body shrink to seventy pounds, as I watched her cheeks hollow, skin yellow, and energy dissipate, I watched her watching me, thinking more of me than the cancerous state of her own body, and I knew that mothering was not just a particular kind of love, not just a selfless and enduring love, and not just a role to be played by an actor. I did not know when I discovered my mother's body in our guest room, lifeless and still, the heat disappearing quickly, how long her love would last.

Is it in every good and dark thing I do?

Our mothers give us life. And death. And longing. And the deepest of our regrets.

And when your mother dies, you feel so sorry for yourself. You feel like crying and you do. And the wail is often a baby's wail. It is, in an adult man, a strange and beastly sound. I roared and I wondered, at the same time, exactly who was roaring.

My wife found me in the basement, lost in a much-needed nap.

"Your mother is gone," she said.

"What?" I said. "No, she can't be."

Then she grabbed me, pulled me down, and sat with me on the carpeted stair to the laundry room. She held me in her arms, as I sobbed and wondered who I was now, now that my mother was gone.

Was I the little boy who misses his mommy, the woman who eternally cheers him, forgives him, and worships him? Was I the adolescent boy who sees his mother as a nuisance, a nosy caregiver, an appendage of his father? Or was I the grown man who sees his mother as his best connection to the past and his best insight into the future?

In the days after her death, I began to fall back to earth. Hours would go by when I didn't think of her. A day would go by and I would have forgotten to think of her. Now it's down to once every couple of days.

I think about my mother. Sometimes when I'm really sick I wish she could come to me in her flannel nightgown, put a cold compress on my forehead and sit on my bed. Sing me a song. Sometimes, for no reason, when I see something beautiful, like the sun, the sky, a mountain, or my daughter's eyes, I want to cry. I want to sob. I feel so sorry for myself. I want to mourn her.

But I am a man without a mother now. I am a man who has lost his mother. I am a man who must go on without his mother's love. So I hold my son and daughter now. I hold them tightly. I hold them secretly when they don't know it. When I hug them goodbye in the morning when they leave for school, I hold them tightly, and I don't want to let them go. I want to fix time, so they do not grow. I want to fix time, so love cannot change.

I want to fix time, so we do not die.

Sometimes I imagine she's watching. But I know my mother is gone, that she does not exist, that I cannot step into the same spot of the river twice. She does not exist. That's what I say. That's what I write.

She is pages in my hand. Pages in my hand. I am afraid to scatter the ashes that sit in the yellow cedar box. She is not scattered. If I let her go, where will I be? The river of love is flowing, calling me to the ocean, where it is warm and salty and crimson, where I can go to sleep and dream of her no more.

The Special Place

If you're already in this special place, you know the truth. All of us, one day will be one of two things: someone who is cared for or someone who does the caring. It is not easy to be in either position. And it's especially tough if you're caught in both positions at the same time.

To be cared for is not easy. Especially at the beginning, all of us have to decide whether we want to accept help. Accepting help requires us to recognize our personal needs and figure out how to deal with the loss of pride and loss of control that may accompany help.

Even when things become very difficult, asking for help seems like a last ditch plea. We tend to wait too long to reach out. We tend to wait too long to tell others that we're tired, worn out, or just in need of a break. We tend to wait too long, and then face caregiver stress and potential burn-out.

Ironically, primary caregivers, those of us who are looking after an ailing child or aging parent, often find it most challenging to turn to others for help. A wife whose husband is seriously ill feels like a failure, even though she knows she needs help with the cooking or the housework. The caregiver faces feelings of guilt even though the work may be overwhelming, even though the resources might be available without cost.

Just before our first child, a boy, was born, we lost my mother to cancer, after caring for her in our home for a year. When our son was a toddler, he began losing his hair and eventually he lost it all. At the same time, my wife's parents both became afflicted with memory loss, dementia, and eventually Alzheimer's. My father had also fallen victim to schizophrenia.

Between young kids, ill parents, and a new marriage, my wife and I discovered what it feels like to be squeezed from all sides.

Caring for someone can be a great joy and a great sacrifice. We become used to the daily rituals, accustomed to the selfless sense of duty, but as our loved one becomes more ill or requires more care, it can be very difficult to share the load.

My wife and I felt important during those years. Our actions felt critical; our senses were continually on high alert. At the same time, we recognized very quickly that we were falling apart. When one of the children would cry at night, we would grit our teeth in anger and frustration. It was three in the morning. Someone would need to wake up soon. We wondered if the tiredness would ever leave our bones.

Eventually, we sought help. Our friends helped us in innumerable ways. The birth of our second child was greeted by an entire community of friends. My mother's funeral was attended by a fleet of home care support workers, hospice volunteers, and medical professionals. My wife's parents' affairs were supported by family members, friends, social workers, nurses, and doctors.

In short, we survived because we accepted help.

Sometimes help was a casserole left at the front door. Or an offer of babysitting combined with movie passes. A ride to the doctor's office. A neighbour mowed our lawn; another shoveled our driveway; another listened to me wail about the unfairness of it all. Even with all this help, we were so worn out that I cannot remember some years. I have a hard time remembering my students during those years. I worked on auto-pilot.

Caregiving is a balancing act. It requires dedication to the loved one, but it also requires a dedication to self-awareness. You need to monitor yourself and understand that if you don't take care of yourself, then the whole system faces jeopardy.

I never realized that taking care of yourself could be so challenging. Eating well, exercising, those things are difficult enough without having to think about one's mental wellness and energy reserves.

I became adept at talking about myself as if I were a car. I needed regular maintenance. I had a gas tank that needed filling, and if I felt like the needle was nearing empty, I immediately tried to find some time for myself, to do those activities that would recharge me, nourish me, and prepare me to be strong.

My wife, who is much stronger than I, more resourceful, and way better at most things, showed me that being a caregiver, despite the stress, despite the exhaustion, can be one of the most rewarding things we ever do.

When you give love without any conditions, it is like your heart muscle expands and your ability to feel the great joys of life are intensified. While I remember the tough times, I mostly remember what I learned, not about myself, but about Beckett, Clementine, Piet, Kayo, Sook, Ji Won, and Alberta.

To give care, to receive care, to support those in need in whatever small way we can, is one of the great rewards of being alive. I never thought that cleaning a toilet, reading to someone, or eating an ice cream cone on a picnic bench — I never thought that these things were really all that important.

I thought my life was to be dedicated to writing books, teaching, and thinking about big ideas. But I was wrong. To love and accept love is more challenging, more creative, and more rewarding than anything I ever imagined.

Thank you to all those who care for others. And to those who accept care, thank you for receiving our care with dignity and understanding.

Statistical Sweet Nothings

We all have a long list of regrets. I regret every mishap, especially car accidents and snowboard crashes where I land on my head and forget things afterward. I regret other things, too — humiliations, embarrassments, and mistakes that play in my head like a pop song from the eighties.

I've made many mistakes with people. As you get older, you try harder to be wise, purposeful, courageous in all that you do. Courageous, not just in the physical sense, but in the sense that we learn to face the things that frighten us.

In the past I have been a coward about many things, skulking out of the room instead of raising my voice. Emotional and intellectual courage is the challenge of a lifetime; it takes guts to face and acknowledge that which triggers your deepest fears. All of us, for example, find it difficult to face personal criticism. Even the strongest must learn to recognize the statistically valid fact that not everyone will agree with us, like us, or respect our point of view.

Being misunderstood is part of life, but accepting that fact isn't the journey of life; nor is the movement from cowardice to courage the journey either. My real problems lie outside my own awareness.

It's no wonder we can feel smug as we grow older. We believe that we are indeed facing down our perceived obstacles, that — yawn — our fears are gradually becoming like comfortable shoes. We are used to being how we are, we accept our nature, and we decide, sooner or later, not to care about that which we do not care about (or even know about).

But perhaps what we don't know about ourselves IS the undiscovered country. After all, often what we do not know informs the opinions of others. You may not know exactly how you may come off to another (and may not care), but that person's view of you should not be ignored, not because you should accept the other's perceptions and judgments, but because you should at least attempt to understand what occurs outside your own awareness and measure this against your own sense of yourself.

Do you know what people really think of you?

You think you know your strengths and weaknesses, but how do you really know? Like all those really bad singers on American Idol, you might be fooling yourself. For example, you might think you're a really great friend, but your friends might not actually think so. You might think that you're generous; others may say that you're always looking for an advantage in your generosity. You may wonder why you don't get invited to many parties; others may say you're competitive, hiding your insecurity. You may think you're a wonderfully curious columnist with a lot on his mind; others may say you've an irritating propensity for introspection as well as bad breath.

I have often thought of myself as the "smart guy" or "the creative guy." But some of my friends disagree. They say I am the "controlling guy," the guy who always wants to drive the bus. How much truth is there in the perception of others? We all know someone who considers themself the honest guy, the one who has the guts to tell it like it is. Well, we all want to tell this person, give it a rest, your famous bluntness is not making you very much fun to work with.

At parties, we all know people who squeal, "I'm a people person," but after you meet them you feel like running for the chip dip. People believe all kinds of things about themselves without ever looking in the mirror of other people's perceptions.

So I have decided to interview my wife. Shouldn't your life partner be able to tell you the unseen truth about yourself?

Me: So, dear wife, how are you?

Her: Okay. You?

Me: I'm okay. Happy to be married, I'd say.

Her: Very funny. What do you want?

Me: I'm doing a column on self-deception.

Her: Right up your alley.

Me: So can I ask you some questions about me?

Her: Shoot.

Me: Why do you love me?

Her: Huh?

Me: Come back here. Sit down. Please ...

Her: You're asking me: Why do I love you?

Me: Yeah.

Her: Well, let me think, I guess it's because of the way you make me feel.

Me: What? You haven't mentioned my soaring intelligence, heightened creativity, unbelievable leadership skills, or the A I got in physical education 11.

Her: My dear husband, I love you because of the way you make me feel, not because of all your accomplishments, trips to Ottawa, or high school report cards.

Me: Let me get this straight. I asked you that question because I wanted to find out something about myself, but instead I find out, and pardon me if this sounds a bit harsh, that the facts of my exist-ence, your judgment of who I am, is simply seen in the inescapable perspective of your own ego?

Her: So?

Me: I don't get it.

Her: Look, honey, instead of giving you some quasi-objective view of you as a jumble of historical, personal and biographical nar-ratives or other ego-gratifying perspectives that I'm sure you'll eat up, I am simply stating that the reason I love you is the way you make me feel.

Me: Really?

Her: Yeah.

Me: No way.

Her: Way.

Me: I don't get it.

Her: Dear husband, you are to me as I am to you. You would not like me, let alone love me, if I did not make you feel a certain way when we are together in the physical sense and beyond. In short, I need you to love me, and most of the time I feel loved.

Me: But aren't my achievements important to you? Why am I putting all this effort in?

Her: Yes. I want to be loved by someone who I respect and admire.

Me: But couldn't you respect and admire anyone?

Her: True.

Me: Then I'm not really all that special in the romantic exceptional sense, but more special in the statistically valid sense that we have enough in common for us to love each other.

Her: You like saying statistically, don't you? It kinda gets me hot.

Me: Am I mister right or mister right here and right now?

Her: Love isn't quite a lottery; it's more like a decision, a deep-seated decision.

Me: I really hate deep-seated decisions. They remind me of deep-seated pants and I am too young for them.

Her: If you say so.

Me: So here I am under this illusion about what makes me special to you and I find out from you that it's all about ... commitment?

Her: It's more than that because the commitment has to be acted on every day. Like when you'll vacuum the house later.

Me: Be serious.

Her: A commitment ONLY means something when you actually do something, whether consciously or not, to make me feel loved, every day.

Me: What?

Her: Sometimes you do stuff that I don't think you're aware of that I absolutely love. I love the way these actions make me feel.

Me: Really? So now, you're finally starting to answer the question: What do you love about me?

Her: Well, okay, if you want to put it that way, but isn't it the same with me? You say that you want to examine the impact of a person's presence outside that person's perceptions, right?

Me: Yeah.

Her: Well, I love the way you care about me, even when all it may mean that day is the way you love our children. I love the way you love others, me included. And how we talk during commercials.

Me: You love the kind of TV watcher I am?

Her: Sort of.

Me: And I love how you make me feel, too. I love how you embrace life.

Her: I love how you see the best in me.

Me: I guess that's why we're together.

Her: Any more questions?

Me: Nope. Walk with me.

Her: Where are we going? Hey, it's not Sunday morning, you know.

Me: I want to show you something deep-seated.

Her: Oh my.

Me: I'll whisper sweet statistical nothings in your ear.

Her: No way.

Me: Way.

Waiting for Beckett

In January of 1997, my wife Alberta and I spent the night in the maternity ward. It was a great night. The birth of our first child went very quickly.

Maybe too quickly. The regular contractions started around 10 p.m. The contractions plateaued about seven or eight minutes apart around eleven, so I went downstairs to watch sports highlights.

We had heard all these horror stories about long deliveries. "Our labour was 14 hours long." "Our labour was 19 years and counting." "Oh yeah, in the play 'Waiting for Godot' he never arrives."

I tried to block it out. Sports highlights are a man's way of relaxing. Cavemen, of course, attended to fire and security. It was the same thing with me in my cave: I needed to attend to the overall se-curity and health of the NHL. At about 11:20 p.m., she gave me the nod. We sped down to the hospital in our new Subaru. I helped Alberta through the twisty cor-ridors of Prince George Regional Hospital. She had to stop and lean against the wall a few times.

"We're not lost, honey. Don't you worry. I'm sure we're not lost."

When we found the maternity ward, the older nurse gave me a glare: turns out Alberta was fully dilated. "Took your time, eh?"

I tried to explain. She frowned. She lectured. I asked for another nurse. This was not easy but it worked. I have what is called in TV cop show parlance good "suction," meaning I can be very convincing if I have to be.

After the delivery, my wife was fine, but she had torn pretty badly. Our baby boy was strong and healthy, although after the delivery both of us nearly fainted during the stitching. There was blood. I remember watching 64 minutes tick off the clock while the doctor worked. She was so pale that it hurt me.

I watched her holding our son and then I watched Dr. Kwan's forehead beading up with sweat; his eyes said that if he stitched fast, things would be fine. The dark and slippery floor. I got dizzy but the curtains helped me stay up. Reciting hockey statistics helped me, too.

Like Stan Mikita scored 1467 points in his career. What a guy. What a name.

On the third day, the nurse showed us how to hit the road. I learned to wrap my son up. Once bundled, he fit nicely in the crook of my arm like a football. He was solid. Nearly eight pounds. Fat cheeks. Covered in tiny spots. Hair all wild over his forehead like a mini-Cro-Magnon man.

Kind of like me.

The nurse showed us how to set him up in the car seat. I concentrated during the lesson. Bringing a kid home from the hospital is serious. You don't want to crash the car and send your first kid, on his first drive, flying through the windshield like a torpedo.

"Listen," the nurse said. "Your wife is going to be in bed for two weeks. You're going to be taking care of the baby."

"No problem."

Let me warn you now about this kind of bush league over-confidence.

They finally released us late Saturday afternoon. Our new split level in the suburbs sat waiting. My wife didn't notice the fresh vacuum marks all over the house. She didn't notice the smell of tuna casserole covered with mushroom soup.

"I just need to lie down," she said.

"Hey, Beckett," I said holding my son. "We waited a long time for you."

That's when I felt this deep low frequency vibration. Perhaps an earthquake had ripped through town? Oh, no. The vibration came from him.

Diaper time. Cottage cheese time. Hold your breath time.

You should know one thing about changing a newborn's diaper. This is true even if the kid has just pooped against the direction of gravity and you're cleaning curds up his back up to his neck. The rule is that a newborn's poop perfume is delightfully wonderful, is nearly consumable — when compared to the diaper of a two year old.

The flashbacks. We will not get into this horror.

After I had cleaned the bum, washed the bum, and covered the bum with goo, I tried snapping up the fancy designer sleeper that my cousin Harold had sent. Not good. I frantically rummaged around our new baby clothing and found this terrycloth bag thing with a head hole, arms, and a drawstring at the end.

Now, this was a piece of baby clothing invented by a man. I needed to get at least thirty of them. I needed to replace the drawstring with one of the cords you see on sleeping bags.

My wife fed our boy in bed. She slept with him a little. I set up dinner. We smiled foolishly at each other. A few nights later, she told me the new deal.

"You're going to sleep with him. In the other room."

"I'll need milk," I said defensively.

"I've already expressed and frozen some."

Now, I'll skip through the stuff that most men have trouble with when taking care of a baby. I've seen guys struggle to make it past the one-hour mark. My advice is that if you can't last an hour with your own kid, you'd better man up and fight through it no matter how much your wife thinks you can't pull it off. Yes, it's overwhelming. Yes, stinky time is stinky time. But the more time you spend alone with your kid, the better.

But sleeping with your baby at night is a different matter. This is what separates the amateurs from the pros. This is where you step it up. This is play-off time, boys.

When your kid cries, usually you look for one thing – the hand off. The key here is not to be afraid of a little crying. Baby crying is baby communicating. It's like learning a new language. You've got to listen and experiment. Some cries mean food. Other cries mean I want to slap the light switch fifty times. Some cries say look at me, hold me close, and make me feel loved.

This last category, in case you didn't know, is the grail, the Stanley Cup. (What a name for a top award.)

Those nights with my baby were some of the best moments of my life. At first, I spent a lot of time wondering what to do about the crying. I couldn't tell if he was hungry or cold or a combination of everything.

I walked around with him on my shoulder. I cleaned his little belly cord with a Q-tip. I sang him songs. When it got late, I made up a little bed on the floor. I stripped off my shirt and held him to my bare chest. I held him tight while he sucked on the bottle. Man, this baby had incredible suction. Kind of like me.

I stared at his tiny face. He was sucking intently. He was curling his toes. Slurp, slurp. I felt something descend onto me. I closed my eyes and let the feeling fill me. He stopped sucking and pushed out the plastic nipple. I picked him up and patted his back until he burped.

I lay down beside him again. I felt an energy flowing through me as I held his body. It took me awhile, after all I am a man, but I knew what this energy was. It was love. I knew it had to be love. I remember feeling like I was sparkling, like I could light up the universe.

This is who I am now, I thought. This is who I am. Your father. Always your father. I'm taking care of you now. It's me and you and the beautiful woman asleep in the next room.

The Brave Heart: How to Say Goodbye

"Never can say goodbye." — THE JACKSONS
"Breaking up is hard to do." — NEIL SEDAKA

One of the things I am trying to teach myself is how to say goodbye. I have taught my kids to say goodbye to their friends by escorting them to the door, looking them in the eye, and sincerely thanking them for the visit. But there is a lot more to goodbye, isn't there?

Farewell soirees, funerals, retirement events, reunions — if you don't like saying goodbye, these events can be uncomfortable.

When you are young, you really don't know how to say goodbye. You mumble some words, shut the door, and turn your back. Then it happens to you. Everybody knows what it feels like when your best friend moves away. You cry in your pillow. You miss them so much. You want to tell them how you feel.

You know something is missing. You want to say goodbye properly. But you don't quite know how.

As you get older, you master different ways of saying goodbye. When I left my family to attend school in Toronto, my sister's way of saying goodbye was awfully simple: she avoided it. I knew she cared a lot.

Lots of people avoid saying goodbye. Who can blame you? It's too painful. You might get emotional. It's much easier to suppress your feelings. It's much easier to say "forget about it."

I think our significant relationships are marked by what we have learned about saying goodbye. If you don't say goodbye properly, let's say you run away, practice avoidance, or lie about your true feelings, one thing is sure: a bad goodbye will follow you.

Like the pop song says, breaking up is hard to do. People who cannot break up properly become imprisoned by their inability to be forthright. When you can't say goodbye, you may not resolve your feelings. Sometimes difficult feelings keep returning to you or you fall into patterns. You wish there was no unfinished business. We all want to move on but sometimes it feels like we're running in place.

Is it wrong to skip goodbye when you no longer want a relationship with someone? For example, a good friend of mine is drifting away. What should I do? Should I let the friendship die a slow death of negligence? Or should I stab the relationship in the heart with a clear and honest goodbye?

"I am finding it hard to be friends with you. We have been friends for a long time but right now it's not working. It's not the same anymore. I find it too difficult to be friends with you. If you're not ready to resolve this, I think it's time to move on."

Now who the heck can say that?

A proper goodbye can change your life for the better. I said goodbye to my parents before each died, and although I was enormously afraid, I said the words I needed to say. If you ever have said goodbye properly, you know how right it feels.

"I love you. I will always love you. You are my everything. If it's okay with you, I think I can let you go now."

My children are at the stage when they are beginning and ending many relationships. I would like my son and daughter to know how to say goodbye in an honest, respectful, and sincere way. Often there is no way to avoid the pain, but there is a way to recognize and respect each person. Easier said than done, right?

Are you like me? Do you have a lot of unfinished business in your life? There are people that I have treated so poorly. I should have been more honest. I should have shown more courage. I should have been braver.

Maturity is a funny thing. How you say goodbye tells you a lot about where you stand on the road of life. Can you be sensitive and honest with someone, or do you bury your emotions and hope they will go away?

Sometimes, when we feel we are wronged, we really want to practice avoidance and justify our denial. Sometimes we say it's not worth it.

It's just not worth being your friend, we say. But what we're really saying is that self-honesty and genuine respect for another person is not worth it.

We all realize, sooner or later, that relationships only grow when we are courageous enough to voice our true feelings. We know that relationships deepen when we work through our grievances, when we express our sincere feelings, when we say how hurt we have been.

When you say goodbye to someone, whether it's for eight hours or forever, you try to express your appreciation for your time together. But most of all, I think, you recognize that life is transitory, anything can happen, that this moment might very well be the last honest moment you have together.

How do you know you have said goodbye properly? How do you deal with the inevitable mourning period when you miss the person even as you are thankful the relationship is over? How do you avoid that seemingly endless make up and break-up cycle?

I don't know.

What I do know is that I still possess wounds from relationships gone by. I still think about my failures, and in this way old wounds sometimes never heal.

Your friend leaves you and this hurts. We cry for many reasons, but the tears of goodbye seem the most potent. I thought when I was a child that death was merely a vacation. You could simply pretend that the person was temporarily gone. How wrong I was.

I also realize that I have always wanted to avoid the pain of goodbye. I have never wanted to confront my own tears. Death is the toughest goodbye of all. There is so much that should have been said. So much that was unsaid. So much that could have been better.

When the tender tears of goodbye flow, if you are strong enough to let them, the tears can heal you.

"I just wanted to say goodbye. I wanted just to tell you how I feel. I wanted you to know how close you are."

Whether you're a young person deciding to break-up with your first sweetheart or a senior who is afraid to go the hospice and say goodbye to a dear friend — every moment is an opportunity to search our hearts for the truth.

What is the truth?

At the same time that we are so easily damaged, so vulnerable to the words and actions of others, we also know that it is our relationships that define us. It is okay to let go of our difficult relationships. It is okay to say goodbye. But how different life would be if we opened our hearts and practiced being brave.

August 2006:
Last Day with Father

Today's the day. Eyes open. Blink. She moves beside me. Blink. Eyes open again. Moments pass. How long? Turn to my side. Stare at the curtains. Light glows behind them. Swing my legs out. Find slippers. Fumble for eyeglasses. Shuffle to the bathroom. Walk down the hallway. Hold my wife between kids, bedrooms. Close eyes. Hold her still. Breathe. Ask how she slept. Look into her eyes.

Today's the day I see my father for the last time.

Load van. Get in. Check list. Turn the key. Return for sunglasses and jackets. Check tires. Watch landscape blur. Westbank. Peachland. Listen to Feist. Coquihalla. Left at Merritt. South. Eyes on road. Cross Port Mann. Enter Burnaby. Park. Ignition off. Deep breath. Back of shirt wet. This is the hospice. All tumble out. Flat low building. Sky. Trees moving in the distance. We wonder.

My daughter, seven, asks, "Do you want me to come with you to see your father, Daddy?" Choking in my throat. Fight back feelings. Be a dad to her.

"I don't know what he'll be like," I say. "Maybe it's better that I go in alone."

"That's okay, Daddy," she says. I take strength from a little girl. "Are you all right?" asks my wife. I brace myself and she holds me. I let out a breath. "Okay, I'm going in. It's only been sixteen years." Time to see him one last time. Time to see him alive. So that I can w The front door is locked. Trick door to stop wandering. A stranger lets me in. Step inside. Inhale. Try not to smell, but it's okay. Look for reception. Light seems golden. Families meet with patients.

Pass a kitchen on the right. Pink cardigans. Nurses talking. August weekends. Stand. Stand some more. They acknowledge me.

"I'm here to see my father," I say.

They've been waiting for me. Seem to know me. They tell me something. I don't tell them I am afraid. I don't show my fear. They tell me something I don't hear. They tell me again. Room number 26. They point to the left.

The hallways are still. I move. Some doors open. Some are closed. People here to die. People here today. Look right. Look left. Here is the door. Pause. Breathe. Breathe again. I knock.

Move in. The bed is alone. New Balance running shoes sit side by side. No him. He might still be in the shower, I remember the nurse saying. I wait. Check watch. Check date. Check myself. I am working. All organs working. For all I know. For all I know.

A man walks down the hall toward me. Hair still wet. Slim. Youthful. Hardly any gray for a man in his seventies. Well-looked after you'd say. Not frightening. Not violent. Any more.

What am I so afraid of? You small little boy. Mental illness works like a preservative on the body, my sister tells me. He doesn't look like a dying man. The stomach cancer is closing off the top of his stomach. His organs are failing.

He looks stranded here in a hospice of dying people. Looks more alive than all of us. "Hello, Dad," I hear myself say. "Do you have time to see me?"

"Come in," he says.

The invitation is polite, courteous. I've forgotten his courtesy. His formality. I walk into his room again. He's wearing plastic slippers. Something for the beach. He points to a chair. He sits on the bed. He looks thin. Black eyes. Bright. Alert. And me? Controlled I am. This is not so bad. So far.

Now this is how it goes.

"Who are you?"

"I'm Stan."

"Stan?"

"Your son. Stan and Heidi. Your children."

"Stan and Heidi." He nods. A memory firing.

"You have children?" he asks.

"Yes. Two."

"How old?"

"Seven and nine. A boy and a girl."

"You live in Prince George?"

"Kelowna now."

"Yes. You came down."

"Yes. We came down."

"Why?"

I freeze.

"To see you."

"Me. Why?"

"Hey, Dad. How are you doing? What are you doing these days?" I am so controlled. So controlled I am.

"Not so good," he says. Points to his stomach. Closes his eyes. He's holding himself together, I realize. His pain.

"My time is up," he says quietly. "It's not long now."

"Are you in pain, Dad?"

"No, it's okay," he gestures with hands. He closes his eyes. He goes away for a little while. A breath. He returns to me, to the present, then fades away. My sister says his organs will shut down soon. It's a matter of time. That's why I'm here. It's a matter of time. Eyelashes flash. Eyes open.

"We're here on vacation, Dad. We're going to Campbell River. Remember Campbell River? We used to camp at Miracle Beach, the provincial park. We stayed there many times. Do you remember? You used to pick oysters at Oyster Bay and eat them raw on the shore.

"Yes, it's coming back." He smiles. "Yes."

We laugh. I laugh with my father.

"I go there now with my family. Just as you did with us every summer." The cycle continues. Good or bad. The wheel turns. Pause. Long pause. Light changes outside. Clouds passing outside. I have a feeling now. No more fear. I move to the bed and sit beside him.

"I should get going now, Dad. If you don't mind. I'd like to visit you again.

"It's okay."

"You drove down?"

"Yeah, it's just four hours."

"Why?"

"You're my father. You're my father."

He looks at me. I face his eyes. Black coals. I cannot bear it. I move my hand to cover his. Hold his hand. Tight.

"It's okay," I say.

He faces me. A sob comes from deep in his throat. He is crying now. I move closer. Hold both his hands. Closer again. Hold his body in my arms. His chest is hollow, like a bird. Ribs so light. So fragile.

"You were a good dad," I say. "You were a very good dad."

I say these words without thinking. No tears from me. Not yet. I will feel this all later, I think. Maybe a year later, I think. I release his body. He stands up. The moment gone.

My father walks me to the door. Plastic slippers on his feet. Courteous again. A different person somehow. I walk slowly. I cannot look at him. I cannot look back. He disappears behind me.

Take a right turn in the hallway. Strides long. Trembling inside. Greet the outside air. See the sky. Hold this feeling before it disappears. Quickly now. Make up a face for my wife, son, and daughter.

Foot plant after foot plant brings me to the van. Lean against it. Wonder. About him. About the colour of the sky. He will die a few days later. Lie down and never rise again. Today's a good day to die, he will tell the nurse. It has been a few years now. I am hiding in these words.

The Body Electric

"Embodiment!" — VIRGINIE MAGNAT
"I sing the Body electric." — WALT WHITMAN
"Your body is a wonderland." — JOHN MAYER

"Do our bodies sing?" I ask the children at dinner and they giggle. "The body is wise," says the yogi. She urges me to stretch and breathe. But I've just finished dinner. My body will sing in the parking lot after yoga.

"The body is wise," says the drama professor. "Know it. Feel your body. Feel the emotion in your pores." I look at the window and see my reflection. The body is strange. The body is a stranger. I awake. The soft paws of an old cat standing upon my head. Hear the purring. My body is sore. The tenseness radiates from the back of the neck upward. I can take a few pills, swallow coffee and face the day, but something makes me want to stop and feel the pain, embrace the pain, wrestle it to the ground, understand its source.

Or do I?

"It must be stress," she whispers, pushing her thumbs into the base of my skull. I feel nothing. The furnace blows. My wife's hair smells like vanilla. "Ow," I say. My body is a stranger. It has its own intelligence, a peculiar intelligence, something beyond me, something beyond what I know.

***

"Sing to me. Sing the body electric."

For some, the western separation between mind and body is a conceptual error, the separation a leftover from the soul/body split, illustrative of Plato, Descartes, and myth. For many, the mind is not something separate from the body. Feel – don't think, feel the body's own consciousness. Feel the body's song. Feel the stress your body absorbs. She whispers, "Feel the water on the moon."

"Hey, stop that," I say laughing. We have a house rule: no tickling allowed. Tickling is dangerous. Tickling is craziness, a kind of abuse in itself.

"Hey," she whispers, "be more conscious, more aware." But she does not speak in words.

"More aware of what?" I ask. I want to know. She comes to me in the mornings, touching the back of my neck. I can feel the curve of her shape. I can feel her breath upon my shoulders. "Who are you?" she asks, and the question makes me shiver.

When she holds me in her arms, I want to let go, as if I am falling into fast waters, the river of a woman's love. Out of control – I want to be. Lost in the embrace of full embodiment – when the mind forgets and the body remembers: this is who I am. More than rising thoughts. This is the skin and body of Stan Chung whom I love.

Does your body love you?

"Who am I?" the mind asks, but the body knows the answer. The body's consciousness says that love is more than a feeling, more than willful commitment, just as nourishment is more than digestion, just as you can see things that cannot be seen.

"Is the body dirty? Is the body riddled with secrets? Is the body a wonderland?" "Yes," she says to me gently, "especially when it is loved properly."

The granular light of 7 a.m. She smiles good morning and locks the door. It is Sunday morning again. Another week. The earth has spun seven times. What does the body say beyond its own fatigue, soreness, and numbness? "I'm tired," the body says. "Take my half-heartedness away."

The imagination wanders. Up the road it is Williams Lake and I'm ten years old. I'm riding my green mustang bike, the wind across my face, my feet in a singular whirl. I am all body. I am all time. I am now and forever.

What is it like when nature touches you? What is her language? What does she say?

You are young and old at the same time. You feel more than friction upon your skin. You feel the heat of someone's touch, the texture of time's caress. You feel a child's lips upon your cheek, your mother's hand pulling you up the steps into the hot air of a Vancouver bus. How does your body feel when it remembers? What does it feel? What does it feel under the Okanagan sky?

My body says you're an old man. Another birthday has passed. My body says hang on, hang on tight, or we'll be forced to let go. All systems – let go. But I want to let go, I think, and my body thinks – spasm. My body thinks – collapse. My body thinks – tears.

Tears? What tears?

Give the body a moment to remember the sadness. The sadness exists – not just because of hurts and mistakes that embody your own history – but the sadness of your beautiful wife whose hair smells of vanilla and grass, your mother Sook Ja whose hair smells of cinnamon and suede, your grandmother Bong Choon whose hair smells of dandelion and sesame and all the faces and scents of the women before and after her.

Did anyone touch my grandmother? Inhale her sesame hair? Did she know love? She took care of us in Seoul, when our parents went to Canada. She told us stories at night about robbers and tigers. She never held me. She never kissed me or caressed me. She was pregnant and abandoned at sixteen. How was her feudal lifestyle embodied in my father and then passed to me, to my own hands, to the way you caress your children, to the way they will caress theirs? Who will be there to tame the fistfuls of grasses marking your grave?

You didn't know you carried the sadness of generations in your bones. You didn't know. You understand now, the body says. The invisible limp, the bowed back, the curved leg – you carry the generations of farmers, abalone divers, and spies.

No wonder the body sings electric — rocketing back and forth through generational time where sadness and joy jump like returning salmon. Open your eyes and see the forgotten scars, bent smiles, lost teeth, broken limbs, gnarled toes, double-sized hearts.

Your family is a body, a beautiful, tragic, and forgotten body. The blood of generations cleanses and boils and remembers what you have forgotten: you stand like the grandfather you never met. Informer. Revolutionary. Peasant.

* * *

Pay attention to body, the body of your life. Be aware of the sound of teeth grinding at night. Heed the muscular request to find joy in movement. Sleep well. Eat well. Drink water passionately. Give compassionately. Love well — with much more than everything you have.

At night your body chases you in a dream. Your body smiles. If she catches you, she may tickle you, make you laugh until you cry, and if you're not paying attention, she just may squeeze the life out of you. Are you ready for your body to love you? Sing, body, sing.

The Glory of the Unanticipated Note

Music is the language of the universe. It brings us together like nothing else. We find joy in music. We find solace, too. Music can bring deep emotional, psychological, and spiritual states that we would otherwise deem unreachable.

What gives music this power?

We can also abuse music (and musicians), as we try to unlock music's mysterious secrets. We ask so much heavy-lifting of music: we ask it to sell products, improve mediocre movies, and bring us sentiment when critical thought is required.

At the same time, we have so many unanswered questions about music.

When my father-in-law's brain was ravaged by Alzheimer's, he could still recognize the saxophone of Ornette Coleman, even when communication and recognition of his loved ones seemed all but impossible.

What happens to the brain when it experiences music?

Daniel Levitin, a neuroscientist from McGill, leads a group of scholars, journalists, filmmakers, and other music "activists" who are asking the big questions about music.

We know now that music is more than just another human language that we can learn like Mandarin or calculus. Some even say that "musicality" exists across species, pointing to the songs of the humpback whale and the complex recursive songs of birds such as starlings.

Scientists have long inquired after the biological purpose for a creature's song. We may even ask ourselves the same question: What role did music play in our evolution?

When it comes to birds, whales, or humans, most bets concerning the evolutionary rationale for music centre on the obvious: sexual selection.

"Billy Jean is not my lover," sang Michael Jackson at the peak of his powers on March 25th, 1983, at the Apollo Theatre. For many of us, Jackson's moonwalk performance was one of the rare moments in our lifetime when we witnessed dance combined with song in an unforgettable way.

After the performance, Jackson received a call from an excited fan named Fred Astaire. Sammy Davis Jr. asked for and received his jewelled, black cardigan. Both figures recognized that Jackson was creating more than music or dance, but culture itself. And in this way, Jackson is more a figure like Muhammad Ali than someone like James Brown.

How do we humans use music? We do not joust and square off with our sexual rivals using guitars as our weapons. On the contrary, our musical figures function as cultural agents of social harmony and innovation. Billie Jean forced white radio to play black songs. MTV changed its format and its understanding of colour-blind audiences.

All this, I admit, is hard to believe today, and Jackson's post-1983 career does not help us.

As a matter of fact, many do not believe music to be very important. Many believe that music is merely background for our romantic escapades. Sure, we use music to mark our important milestones; we use music to remember, in Barbra Streisand's words, "the way we were," but Billie Jean reminds us that music is about far more than filling up an iPod with tunes.

The messianic quality to the Billie Jean performance propelled Jackson to global stardom, changed how music was packaged and sold, but more importantly, and this is interesting to think about, Billie Jean was heard in every country, on every radio, and was danced to in every club.

Okay, but so what?

Famed writer and researcher Oliver Sacks has hypothesized that our brains have much more musical capability than we might imagine. In his book *Musicophelia*, Sacks goes as far as to say that humans are primarily a musical species.

Why are we musical? Is it to sing hymns at church? Is it to listen to eighties hits at lunch?

Could the outcry upon the death of Michael Jackson hint at the enormously unconscious but nevertheless central role that music plays in our lives?

The role of music in the evolution of the human species has nearly everything to do with culture-making. Music brings people together in ways that other activities do not.

As of 2003, Sting was making $2000 a day in royalties for the twenty-year-old song "Every Breath You Take." That's about a buck a breath. Not bad for one song.

We may value music (despite our illegal downloading), but we also don't realize the full value of music as a shaper and definer of culture. We think of music as disposable. We would rather our children grow up accountants or engineers than musicians, and we think of musical education as somewhat less important than other "core" subjects.

There are many reasons to take music lessons: to be cool, to have fun, to delight in the notes themselves, but there is more and more evidence that says musical people are better at mathematics, better at spatial thinking, and better at creative problem solving.

Music doesn't just form the soundtrack of our lives; it may be life itself. When I think of all my favourite people in the world, I note that many of them are either musicians themselves or deeply passionate about music.

Why do you like music? Music doesn't just give you a discriminating ear, but it also offers your brain a singular kind of "deep" workout.

Listening to music is essentially about recognizing patterns. In music that interests us these patterns challenge and delight. Music creates patterns but then uses these same patterns to set up the glory of the unanticipated note. Neuroscience says our brains are "plastic;" thus, we can change our brains through the most difficult and complex human activity of all: performing music.

Most pop music is based on a three-chord structure derived from the blues which is the musical genre created at the end of the 19th century by African-Americans. Nearly every pop song on the radio has both a simplicity and a seemingly infinite complexity.

Even physicists who investigate black holes, quantum matter, and string theory posit the musical nature, not just of humanity, but of the universe itself. String theory, as opposed to traditional physics, suggests that matter is not made of particles but of strings that vibrate.

How cool is that?

So music is not just music. Michael Jackson is not just another tragic figure. In his music and in all great music, we have an opportunity to celebrate and unite as human beings and as fellow beings in the universe.

That the essence of life is filled with vibrations that can make us "dance, shout, shake our bodies down to the ground" tells us something about what ought to matter most.

There is no culture on this planet that is not musical. There is no soul on this planet who is not musical. In 1983, there was no music that brought more people together than that of Michael Jackson. To celebrate him is to celebrate music. To celebrate music is to celebrate the closeness of all things.

Maryfield, Saskatchewan – Part I

"Are we there yet?" my little sister asked.

My parents didn't answer. We had just entered the town of Swift Current, Saskatchewan, and we were all exhausted.

I looked around for any fast moving water and then shook my head.

"So much for Swift Current."

My sister held her doll in one hand and leaned her head against the glass. The town was small and soon we were staring at fields of wheat once again. It was mid morning. We passed other towns: Chaplin, Caronport, and Moose Jaw.

"Are we there yet?" I asked just after we passed Regina. My mother threw the map at me.

"Be quiet. We're almost there," my mother said.

"What this for? I don't know how to read it," I pleaded.

"Yobo, you need to turn right in about three hours. Then we go up a dirt road. The town should be about thirty miles off the highway."

"Yobo" is what Korean women call their husbands. First names are never used.

"Okay," my father grunted. At least they were talking. Back in Alberta, he pulled onto the shoulder and ripped the map away. This happened on all our trips.

In protest, my mother put her feet up on the dash and fell asleep. Then, we'd pull into a gas station and my father would force my mother to get directions. And then he would argue with her.

"Are you sure that's right?"

"Aren't you capable of getting directions?" she would ask. Then my father's ears would turn red, and we'd plug our ears.

The TransCanada, the highway we were traveling on, was so straight through the prairies that you could fall asleep at the wheel and be safe for miles. That's what our friends told us in Vancouver, and I couldn't wait to see if was true.

My sister and I watched the never-ending white line that snaked down the middle of the road. We counted the little ponds beside the highway with cattails and red-winged blackbirds. We had contests on who could hold their breath the longest. We begged our mother for candy. We counted birds on fence posts. We sang songs and made funny sounds and panted for the windows to be opened. We stared at the back of our father's head. Then we stared at the back of our mother's head. We noticed that you could see the weather coming from miles ahead. In the distance, clouds billowed upward and grew into thunderheads. We'd lose our concentration and glance elsewhere, and soon, we could see it raining from at least a hundred miles away. The sky seemed so vast and large. We couldn't wait for the rainbows.

I love you Saskatchewan!

My sister and I believed we were on a tremendous adventure. We pretended our car was a soaring magic carpet. I was a prince. She was a princess, and we were looking for Ali Baba's secret caves. My mother, for some reason, could recite many stories from the Arabian Nights. We floated down the highway on our German engineered magic carpet.

Our car quickly became our family's sanctuary, a place of togetherness and privacy, a place of protection and independence. The car remained our protection from the strange and bewildering place known as Canada and the strange and fascinating people known as Canadians.

Almost every Sunday, after church, we would go for a drive. Once church was finished, my father stripped off his sparkling white clerical collar and started up the car. My mother would take us from our play and usher us inside. We knew our father was restless. The church service was finally over. His sermon had been delivered. Hands had been shaken. Hymns had been sung. The offering had been counted.

We'd jump into the car and my father would drive and drive, as if we were never coming back. We would pass houses then farms, and then we'd forget where we were. Fences, cows, birds – they all seemed slightly unfamiliar. The aspen seemed to bend slightly differently in the wind. The rye grasses in the medians appeared a different shade of green. Then, in about an hour or two, my father would sigh, look at my mother, pull over and turn around, our Sunday afternoon mini-vacation finally over for another week.

In 1968, as a present to himself for finally passing his British Columbia driving exam, my father dropped nearly $5000 dollars on a beige Mercedes-Benz 220. It had 118 horsepower, four cylinders, and four-speed manual transmission. At that price, he might have easily purchased a small house near the University of British Columbia, which would be worth many times that now, but my father wasn't that sort of a person.

He bought the Mercedes with the last of the savings from Korea, and he drove it proudly for over twenty years. He drove across the prairies to Maryfield, Saskatchewan. He drove it through intense winters, over gravel roads, and up creek beds on his fishing adventures. That car was my father's baby. His clergy classmates looked at the car when he parked it at the family residence for the first time. They noticed the famous chrome-three-star hood ornament, and they shook their heads with amusement.

"Are you kidding me, man," a fellow minister from Jamaica said. "You're a bloody Marxist, atheist, intellectual. You can't be driving around in that contraption. You need a bicycle, man. Not the bourgeois vehicle of post-Nazi Germany!"

They didn't understand that when he was in Korea, his chauffer drove a Mercedes. As a military intelligence officer and as a member of the KCIA, Mercedes was the only choice. They didn't understand that for my father there could be no other car.

In fact, almost all the toy cars I was given during that time were also Mercedes. Yes, even the five-year-old minister's kid drove a bourgeois vehicle of post-Nazi Germany.

"I love Mercedes!" I used to shout to the kids whose fathers drove Ramblers and Torinos. I used to shout "I love Mercedes," to any kid who challenged me in the sandbox with their love of Dodge Fargos, Scout Internationals, or Ford F150s. Nobody knew what I was talking about.

Now driving a Mercedes down a gravel road in small-town Saskatchewan is a pretty strange thing for a Korean family to be doing in the early seventies.

My mother who spoke only basic English, seemed to enjoy the cross-country drive, but she didn't enjoy having to read the map. She also liked to feed my father while he was driving. It felt pretty intimate to us the way she would force rice into his mouth while traveling seventy miles an hour. We would look away and giggle.

By the time we found the exit and had traveled for twenty minutes on the bumpy gravel road toward Maryfield, my mother truly believed we had dropped off the face of the earth.

"My God," she whispered, as we pulled into the small prairie town, complete with two red grain elevators, a wide main street, and small houses with white picket fences. Behind many of the houses stood lush vegetable gardens with tall, swaying sunflowers and rows and rows of corn. The place felt overgrown, compared to the dry and dusty wheat fields that surrounded the town.

It was the summer of 1970. It had taken us three days to drive half way across Canada to reach my father's first real job in Canada.

He would be the United Church Minister of Maryfield, Saskatchewan, a little town of 750.

My father, ever the wanderer, chose Maryfield because it was far away. He had graduated at the top of the class at UBC's divinity school. Pretty good for a guy who couldn't speak English when he arrived in Canada. But rural Saskatchewan was not his first choice. Other churches had turned him down after the interview. Most churches wanted someone a little more conventional.

Maryfield was good enough to hire him without an interview, so neither party knew what they were getting into.

I don't believe the small town had ever seen a Mercedes-Benz sedan. I don't believe anybody in town had ever seen a Korean, let alone a Korean United Church minister who couldn't speak English without quoting Heidegger. We eventually found the right street and pulled up next to the small tidy church. It was partly brick, partly sided with freshly painted wood siding. It had a small steeple with a bell in it. The cemetery next to it was green and freshly mowed. A white fence surrounded it. The concrete steps looked well swept and cared for. My father turned into the parking lot, turned off the Mercedes, and we climbed out.

I knew my father was nervous. He had been yelling at my mother about her lack of map-reading skills. My mother was doing her best to ignore him. He also didn't enjoy the gravel road coming in. Our precious car was jostled mercilessly, and now it was covered in prairie dust. One Mercedes shock absorber, imported from Germany, would cost $100. My father's salary was $9000 a year.

My sister stretched and pulled her doll out of the car. I looked around with my hands in my pockets and wondered if there were any kids around.

"Reverend Chung?" someone called. It was an elderly man wearing overalls and smoking a pipe.

Maryfield, Saskatchewan – Part II

"The name is Lawrence Johnstone," he held out his right hand. "You must be Sook. And this must be Stanley and Heidi. Pleased to meet you. Welcome to Maryfield. We're so glad to see you."

"Hello," my father smiled. "Are we really here?"

"You are, indeed, sir. You are here."

"I see," my father laughed. "You see," he said to my mother in halting English. "We are here."

"Hello," my mother said, reaching out her hand. "We are here."

"Well, isn't that perfect," said Larry Johnstone.

I looked at my sister and rolled my eyes. My parents possessed extremely sub-par, small talk ability.

My father, I have always thought, possesses a small talk handicap. He simply cannot do it. Ask him about Trotsky. Ask him about Erasmus. Ask him to cast Jesus as a Marxist rebel. Ask him about the necessity of doubt. But don't ask him to small talk.

"So how was the weather on your drive?" asked Larry Johnstone.

"We are here," my sister and I said in unison.

We wondered if maybe they'd change their minds and send us back to Vancouver. Larry Johnstone was head of the search committee. He walked us two blocks over to the manse, the house reserved for the minister.

"Here she is," he said.

He put his hand on my father's shoulder, and you could see my father recoil slightly. Korean men do not touch each other until they've had a lot to drink, and then, and only then, all touching is limited to profuse backslapping.

"Here you are, little lady. It's a little run-down. We haven't had a minister here for some time, so the place will need a bit of airing out. I'm sure you'll manage."

"I see," my mother said, nodding her head. We opened the front door and walked through the living room. The house smelled musty and there was a sour odor. The living room was carpeted. The kitchen and hallway were covered in linoleum squares. My parents stood inside the house wondering whether to remove their shoes.

A family of mice ran across my mother's toes. She was wearing red sandals at the time.

She screamed and scrambled out of the house.

We played in the backyard while my father tried to coax my mother back into the house. She walked up and down the street. My father went back to the church and got the car. He started unpacking the trunk. My mother showed up and stepped into the Mercedes, locked all the doors, and sat there.

My father stood on the steps looking at my mother. Her arms were crossed, and you could tell she had been crying. He pushed us inside and closed the front door. We explored the house while my father sat at the kitchen table staring at his hands.

It was getting dark, so my father walked to the grocery store and bought some Wonder bread. My sister and I sat in the living room looking for mice and dropping bread crumbs. He told us to stop and brought out a few mice traps he had bought at the store.

He told us the traps were dangerous. While he was trying to figure out how to set the trap, it snapped his fingers.

I elbowed my sister and grinned. Then we ran to the window, opened the olive curtains, and check on the status of our mother. She was still there. But she wasn't moving.

My father went out to the car and tried to reason with my mother. She had locked the doors, rolled up the windows, and fallen asleep.

My sister and I could hear our father talking quietly to my mother.

"The neighbours are watching us," he said quietly. "I can see them peering out of the windows. What must they think of us?"

"My mother mouthed something which we couldn't hear, but it wasn't very nice because my father raised his fist. But he wasn't going to hurt his precious car; we knew that for certain.

"I'll clean up the house. I'll get the mice out. Tomorrow, some people are coming with new furniture. Please come out. At least give us the sleeping bags, so the kids can get to sleep."

Eventually my mother opened the door of the car. My father said nothing to her. He just gave her space. She came into the house, and we hugged her with all our might.

"Mommy, there is a big garden out back," said my sister.

"Mommy, there is a huge basement," I said. I don't think the animals are that big down there." She looked up at my father. He was locking the front door. He stood there with his arms crossed.

My mother finally laughed. We went to their bedroom where my father had set up air mattresses. She put our sleeping bags between us and our father, and we listened to the wind rustle through the trees until we finally fell asleep.

Field Trip of a Lifetime

The Governor General's Canadian Leadership Conference attempts to bring together emerging leaders. Every four years, the Governor General and her legion of big-time sponsors put together an event that brings together 200+ attendees chosen from a broad cross section of Canadian society. Each participant chooses a province and undertakes an intense study tour of a province or region. This year, I was fortunate to be chosen.

I selected the province of New Brunswick because I knew nothing about it and because it was far away. You might not be able to tell by looking at me, but I'm a western boy through and through. I grew up in Williams Lake, a barefoot hunter and fisher, and I spent most of my adult life in Prince George, whooping it up on George Street with the two-steppers and displaced forestry workers.

Our tour of New Brunswick brought me shoulder to shoulder with a fascinating cross section of New Brunswick society. My group of fifteen high-functioning, A-types was comprised of politicians, lawyers, unionites, executives, and government types like me. During our encounters, we had a difficult time pulling our punches, even though we were supposed to appreciate and learn, not play the role of advisor or advice-giver.

I dined with the New Brunswick Lieutenant Governor and his partner as our group peppered him with questions about aboriginal economic development. We lunched with the Premier, the Minister of Education, CEOs of two major companies (Moosehead and Ganong), and we never failed to ask the kind of blunt questions reserved for those who are both young, wise, and a little over-exuberant. It didn't take long for our group to call into question our exuberance, retract our collective claws, and begin intensely focusing on a unique brand of appreciative inquiry.

We slept in university dorms, travelled around in a bus, and managed to work from 6 a.m. to midnight most days. We visited a heart-breaking, inner-city school in Saint John which had a multi-generational form of poverty I had not experienced before. We sat cross-legged in the dawn for a two-hour pipe ceremony in the bur-geoning aboriginal village of Red Bank, home to the Metapanagiag people. This was the day of the Canadian government's official apol-ogy. For many of us, this was a transformational day. We cried, we hugged, we bonded, and we committed ourselves to this people who re-discovered their ancestral identity through the discovery of his-torical ruins on the banks of the Miramichi River.

Most every evening, we gathered together to pour out our discoveries and thoughts. We sat in a circle and listened. We found our-selves intensely concerned with the fortunes of this small province, its challenges neatly mirroring the challenges of our country. New Brunswick is facing the exodus of its traditional employers such as the forest products industry. It must deal with both economic and cultural issues, from the diversification of its industrial base to the development of its French immersion educational programming.

It is an energetic province, set in a historically and culturally rich land, where the Acadians, a group of French settlers who arrived in the eighteenth century, dance to a pulse that is at once proud of its resistance to the forces of assimilation, and challenged by the Anglophone traditions of Fredericton, Saint John, and elsewhere.

I didn't know much about the Acadian spirit that resides in the Atlantic provinces, but I admire it so much now. In contrast, the West seems like an adolescent, still struggling as we are with forging an identity based primarily on economic fortunes. In BC, we worry about job. In New Brunswick, a job isn't who you are. The more people I met, the more I fell in love with the New Brunswick people, their honesty, their pride, and most of all, their joy.

Our group felt this joy and rode it like a surfer riding a once-in-a-lifetime wave. I was changed in so many ways during this field trip that I scarcely know how to describe my feelings. From the people of Red Bank, we learned about true authenticity of spirit that is not only grounded in a respect for the past, but a reverence for intimacy, for the space that exists between us. This aboriginal group, led by astonishingly accomplished leaders like Pam Ward, taught us how to embrace one another with an open-heartedness and a vulnerability that, I must say, frightened me to the core.

If you ask the people who know me, they will tell that I'm not exactly a "huggy" kind of person. I've always thought of hugs as slightly insincere expressions of familiarity, but I know now that I couldn't have been more wrong. The people of Red Bank taught me that an embrace can change your life if it is done with an authentic heart and without fear. I cried many times on this trip, and really, I don't know how to tell you about it.

Okay. I know what you're thinking: Stan went on a 15-day multi-million dollar spree to Banff, New Brunswick and Ottawa, and now he says that basically he learned how to hug. How ridiculous. How touchy-feely. How stupid. What kind of leadership experience is that? Yeah, I hear you.

Our goal, at the end of the study tour, was to present our findings to the Governor General herself. Most study groups faced this daunting task at the last minute, producing conventional, rather yawn-inducing PowerPoint presentations that merely skimmed the surface of their provinces. Our group did something quite a bit different. We presented a six-scene, dramatic recreation of the struggles those in New Brunswick face. Our presentation was hailed by some as the best presentation given in the last twelve years. Others were shocked by its raw emotion and ambiguity. Some disagreed with its point of view.

I only wanted to know what SHE thought: Michaëlle Jean, Canada's charismatic Governor General, who watched us carefully and tearfully while we presented. I know this because I was the only one not on stage, for I had the privilege of directing our presentation.

Her Excellency responded by immediately inviting our group to a private lunch. The New Brunswick study group responded by nominating me as the person to sit beside her. I tried to do justice for Pam Ward by advancing the cause of the 400 aboriginals who live on the banks of the Mirimichi River. Her Excellency listened to our stories and honoured our group by praising us for our sense of drama, emotional vulnerability, and originality.

In this majestic conference filled with accomplished leaders, I would say that our group took our lessons to heart and creatively expressed ourselves as Canadians and global citizens. We love this country, but we know that greatness comes from how high we can raise those who are most vulnerable, most challenged, most left behind.

We spent the last three days in Ottawa, sipping Okanagan wine in spectacular settings such as Parliament, the Museum of Civilization, Rideau Hall, and the National Gallery. I was fortunate enough to spend a few more moments with our superstar-like Governor General, but my group knew that I was not totally satisfied with our victory.

"We know what you want," said my friend Naheed, a Harvard-trained activist and academic. "It's not enough that we have this great victory and once-in-a-lifetime learning, you want something more, don't you?"

"I don't want to talk about it," I gulped.

Later on that evening, our last evening, after appetizers and dinner, my group, functioning as a crack team of commandos, helped lead me within striking distance of her through a series of moves and countermoves, until I was maneuvered to the left of one burly bodyguard, to the right of another, and then directly opposite.

And then, there I was face to face with her smiling visage and pulsating figure, with eighties music thumping like my heart throughout the National Gallery, my face frozen in a foolish grin, my A-team laughing and pointing at my ridiculous undulations.

"Look at that idiot," I could hear the union leader from Saskatoon say, "he's dancing, he's getting down, he's boogying with the Governor General of Canada."

Intimacy: Let It Out or Keep It In?

Draw a line on a page. Put some dots on that line. Call it a life line. Instead of mapping out the all-too familiar dates such as your first kiss, your first marriage, your first child, your first gray hair growing out of — forget these milestones — think instead of the most intimate moments of your life.

Intimacy comes in all forms, all shapes and sizes, all flavours and sounds. It is what we fear most, what we prize in our relationships, and what causes many of us the greatest pain.

Intimacy is part of the process of getting to know someone, including yourself, and when we engage in that process, we face moments of doubt, vulnerability, fear, shame, and sometimes great — how does one say it?

Yes, great joy.
I know a man who told his wife every day that he loved her. One time, I was staying at his house and heard the manner in which he said the words.

It is breakfast. She is at the sink in her velvety robe. Although he is long-retired, he is dressed smartly. His tall form approaches her from behind. He puts his arms around her and whispers something I strain to hear.

I can see her knees give a little. I can see his hand slip inside the robe. I turn my head away, and then I hear them talk.

You're my baby, she says.

You're my gold, he says.

And then she makes this R-rated purring sound. It comes from the bottom of her chest. Then I hear a very light kiss.

I love you, he whispers.

A year later, he died of a heart attack. His daughter told me that even on that day, he spoke those three words. He never missed a day.

What do you whisper every day? At my house the refrain is very clear: "What's for dessert?"

After decades of marriage, after everything a couple goes through, how do you say those words so that they remain not only true, but precious, singular, intimate?

Friendship is often where we learn this kind of intimacy. We whisper our secrets. We reveal our desires. But even in friendship it is how we handle conflict that defines the level of intimacy.

The more you tell the truth, the more you fight, sometimes, if you're lucky, the closer you become.

Few people have seen me cry. I do not cry easily because I find it difficult to let myself go. Something inside of me feels locked. I have wondered why it is that I can't feel. Then someone at a dinner party told me: you're a man, you idiot.

Of course, you can't feel, she said. You've spent your whole life being socialized not to feel. Men suppress feelings. To be a man means you let nothing touch you. How can you feel a woman's caress if you've trained yourself since pee-wee to take a cross-check to the face?

It makes sense, but I question this stereotype of men because my male friends are a bunch of highly sensitive, crybabies, who are always talking about their feelings.

One of my toughest friends (I know this because he survived a vasectomy reversal with no anaesthesia) cried for months when his son went away to school.

Hey, dude, how's your son?

Waaaaaa.

I have few male friends who fit the unfeeling stereotype. All it takes is a few beers to get the stories started. Life is hard. The economy is tough. Bosses are bastards. The honey to-do list seems never-ending. Is this all there is to life, some of them ask.

Is this what we signed up for?

In my university days, I gathered my friends at night, forced them to head for one of those beautiful, late-night, Chinese restaurants on Hastings, and we would eat crispy chow mein, drink fresh soy milk, and talk about life's philosophical conundrums.

Okay, mainly we would talk about women.

Now, it is thirty years later, and we are still puzzled by the same questions: how do you get really close to someone? How do you keep a relationship evolving so that it becomes deeper and more meaningful? What do you do when you have gas during yoga class?

Let it out or keep it in?

Homework question: For many couples the first fart is more intimate than the first kiss. Why is that?

Actually, there are two types of men. Those who go to yoga, and those who will never go to yoga. I'm kind of in-between. I have been to yoga, but I find the experience awkward, embarrassing, and just plain uncomfortable — and I'm just talking about choosing the clothing.

Peak experiences of intimacy — if you must know — often occur in alignment with the body. The body recognizes intimacy. Whether it's a moonlit kiss, a Facebook confession, or the curve of your cobra pose, your body knows everything.

The body is wise. Kind of like Santa.

It knows whether you've been good or bad. It knows when you've been naughty. How do you know you've done your body wrong?

Do you have a sore back? High blood pressure? Tense around the neck? Trouble sleeping? Is your stool nicely coiled or does it resemble modern art?

Your body is actually your number one instrument for intimacy. Your eyes. Your hands. Your mouth. Your hips. The way you hold someone's face when you kiss them. The lingering embrace you offer. The arm around a pal's shoulder.

A helping hand.

Intimacy is heightened sharing. It's saying something to someone that melts the glacier, creates momentum, edges humanity forward. It should make your heart beat faster. It should make you wonder if you've crossed the line.

I don't know about you, but I would rather cross a few lines in my life than wonder what might have been. Here are some words that might help you cross the line:

I want to tell you something I've never said before.

I did this for you and you only.

I like this about you.

You make me feel like a monkey.

I want to do something just for you.

Lick me.

I don't think you realize just how attractive you are.

I love the way I feel in your underwear.

Stand in the light just that way, please. No, the dim light.

Yes, I will buy ten copies of your forthcoming book.

Go outside! Let us breathe in here, please.

Stampede Boy

In 1971, when I was eight years old, my parents told us we were moving from our two-bedroom apartment at UBC to the small interior town of Williams Lake. Our parents waddled down the stairs carrying suitcases and boxes. My father loaded the car up. My mother placed a large red metal cooler in the middle of the backseat.

"Be good," she said in broken English. "Cold drink here and lots of food."

My sister and I tumbled into the Mercedes with our pillows. Heidi had her crayons and colouring books. I had my twin holsters and six-guns. I wanted to be prepared; after all, we were headed for stampede country.

We followed the Fraser River, passed sawmills in New Westminster, corn in Chilliwack, and the rafting tour signs at Hell's Gate. We gasped and held our breaths through tunnels with funny-sounding historical names like the long curved one, China Bar.

I figured out by reading tourist signs during roadside breaks that many Chinese worked during the Fraser Canyon and Cariboo gold rushes of the mid-1800s. Nobody in the car was much interested in the pioneers of yesterday.

We were the pioneers of the 1970s. I knew we would be the only Korean family in town and that my father would be the first and probably last Korean United Church minister in Williams Lake.

We drove onto a plateau and into the dry country around Cache Creek. The sky was wide and blue.

"Hey, those look like tumbleweeds," I said.

"Just like on Bugs Bunny and the Road Runner," my sister said. My mother ignored us, held the map in her lap, and concentrated.

"Yobo," she said in Korean, "don't turn toward Kamloops or we'll end up in Saskatchewan where I spent two unbearable winters."

"Maryfield, Maryfield, we love Maryfield," we yelled in unison.

We gassed up and stopped for pie and coffee at a place in Cache Creek called the Wander Inn. The owners were Chinese, a small balding man and a sturdy woman with two bespectacled daughters. They looked at us. We looked at them.

"Japanese?" The man said as he filled my father's cup with coffee.

"Korean," my father said. The man smiled but I could tell he was disappointed that we couldn't speak their language. The two girls glanced at us shyly. Their eyes were shiny stars on a black sky.

I woke up suddenly as my father backed the car into our new home in Williams Lake. The air was cool and the sky was purple. We stood in the grass field beside the church, looking at our first house. The minister's manse was right beside church. It was across the street from the War Memorial Gym. Across from the church was an elementary school, Marie Sharpe Elementary.

Our mother made our beds and pinned up towels as curtains. My bedroom sat at the back of the house, overlooking an elm tree and the dirt driveway. The elm tree is a favourite memory. Its leaves shimmered in the wind at night. Green light filtered into my room in the morning. I will always love elms.

The next morning, I found three Uncle Ben's beer bottles on the front yard. A cocker spaniel watched me from the house beside us. Our yard was overgrown with dandelions.

"Hey, dog," I said.

My father took the bottles and told me that the bottles were donations from people who enjoyed the stampede the previous week. Across the street, I watched a large pile of snow melting beside the rink. In the distance, high on a hill, I could see what was probably the hospital. I put my hands in my pockets and headed for the school playground.

It wasn't very long before Williams Lake became my home. People generously invited us to their homes. We shook hands and smiled and nodded furiously. After church, people came over and sat on our dusty old furniture, drank tea and ate little cookies with a red centre which we were not allowed to have.

People patted my head and told me I looked kind of like an Indian with my blunt bangs, white teeth, and dark skin, so I tried to make friends with First Nation boys, but most of them lived on the reserve, so I made friends with the boys and dogs in the neighbourhood. I rode my bike – everywhere – downtown, deep in the bush, to South Lakeside which even today is a pretty long bike ride for a boy.

It didn't take very long for me to become a stampede boy. I knew how to jump a motorbike, fly down the wing and wind up for a slap shot, catch trout barehanded, cuss, toss cow pies, fire a 12 gauge, and dodge knives. I threw rocks at cars, ran from storekeepers, and played spin the bottle with the older sisters of the girls I knew. I played outside all the time, and I would come in after dark, my face shining with heat, ready on a Sunday night to watch Walt Disney, the Waltons, and endure a shallow, weekly bath.

Soon I discovered that every Chinese restaurant seemed to hold a cute little daughter that would look at me with an air of distant familiarity. There was pretty Jean from Sam's restaurant. And glorious Janet from the restaurant downtown. I would sit on my mustang bike outside these restaurants, with my thumbs in my Lee jeans, my jacket billowing with the wind, and my heart furiously beating.

Williams Lake will always be a wonderful place for me. I still go into town whenever I pass by. The town has changed so much, but the lake is the same, Scout Island is the same, Fox Mountain is the same, and a part of me is the same.

With my family in tow, I like to show my children where I played, where I ran, where I skated, where I came into my own as a Canadian boy.

The manse and church are long gone. So is Sandy, the cocker spaniel next door. So is most everybody. But sometimes I am surprised. My father is still remembered at the church. My mother's kindness is still recalled.

The boys and girls I knew in Williams Lake have their own families now; many left town after high school or even earlier. The painful legacy of the residential schools continues. Many people, like my favourite teacher Frank Trenouth, boyhood idol Brent McDonald, best friend Andy Gibbs, have moved to the Okanagan, and I'm always pleased to see that the Willie's puddle families are doing well, surviving, and moving forward.

The scent of sweet and sour pork on skin, the dark elm-shaded window of an old manse, a rainbow jumping in a blue lake – there is always something that pulls me toward Williams Lake. Perhaps it is the innocence of youth or the memories of my many adventures or how it felt to be a family growing up as one, pioneers in a strange and beautiful place that I will always call home.

Vacation from Vacation

It's vacation time, and I'm failing again. I can't relax in traditional ways, and my vacation is slipping into a "stay-cation," because every time we go somewhere – camping at Mabel Lake or touring Nelson – I end up needing a vacation from my vacation.

I suspect that it's my warped personality that keeps me from enjoying my time away from work, but I have other theories where it's somebody else's fault.

My first theory is that we don't have enough vacation time in the calendar to be any good at it. European countries have much longer mandated vacations (4-6 weeks is the norm, and France has a 35-hour work week). The most successful vacation I've ever had lasted about three days.

True, I didn't have time to get bored or tired. But it's also true that three days is the length of our long weekends, and we Canadians are pretty good at taking advantage of our long weekends. Three days is too short to drive very far or spend a lot of time on a flight, so we are purposely modest and realistic about what we can achieve on a long weekend.

But give me one, two, or three weeks, and I fall apart. Long vacations cause me to panic because I want to pack in "value." I want to see how far I can go, how many Air Miles I can accrue, and how many activities I can squeeze in. I end up returning home un-rested, unrelaxed, and unhappy.

After we get home, I almost always think to myself that the true purpose of a vacation is to make yourself appreciate your humble home.

I guess that's why Canadians love to travel. We love to go on cruises, rack up the kilometres, and stroll the boardwalks of foreign locales. We are camping less, flying more, and even putting our vacations on our 29.9% department store credit cards.

What is so wrong that we are so desperate to get away?

Judging by the line-ups at the Kelowna Airport, we must have it really bad. Just as tourists arrive in littering, butt-flicking, beer-smashing hordes, we can't wait to get the heck out of here.

Even paradise can grate on the nerves.

I am one of those Okanagan clichés that loved vacationing here so much that I ended up staying. I still tend to visit places that I could theoretically move to. That's why I am one of those idiots that realtors love to hate: I look at real estate when I'm on vacation, and I'm not just talking about time-shares. I think I actually go on vacation as some kind of wonky cultural anthropologist because I'd rather experience living in a place than sit at the hotel pool reading a Grisham thriller.

We've had a ton of out-of-town visitors lately (who hasn't?), and I always ask visitors where they would live if they wanted to write, eat, and live really cheaply but still be surrounded by beauty and culture. Last year, people were telling me it was Portugal; the year before, central Mexico; and now the hot place, at least in my mind, is Malaysia.

Why do I want to live for a while in Kuala Lumpur? Three words: 80-cent lunch. I could get a lot of work done in a modern city where I could eat for 80 cents.

There's that word again: work. I'm one of the numbskulls who'd rather write an essay than tan on the beach. I'd rather cycle up Knox Mountain than stroll the sidewalk eating ice cream. And debating the merits of a foreign film with my witty wife is a lot more fun to me than riding upside down in a roller coaster. (Okay, call me an über nerd.)

Vacation, work, vacation, work — to me the words are really not that different. In fact, I've even coined the phrase "work vacation" to explain to my wife how I want to stay home from my job, but write ten hours a day. It's work, but it's fun, I struggle to explain.

"You mean," my wife says, "it's work for us, but a vacation for you."

We all have activities that are creative and challenging and beautiful to us and ONLY us. When we engage in these activities a lot of nutty science fiction-like things happen: we lose track of time, we feel inspired, we feel super energized and strong, as if we were doing the naughty Tour de France or Barry Bonds thing.

Doing something you love ought to be what you do on your vacation.

But instead, we chase wasps around the picnic table or sit in five-hour ferry line-ups or stub our toe during midnight journeys to the outhouse or blow thousands on package vacations where we come home totally drained or worse yet — no different than when we left.

How did your last vacation change you?

I'm considering giving up the notion of vacation. My friend Peter believes in the "stay-cation." For Peter this is when you toddle around the house in ritualized glory while barring the door to guests who insist on bringing their friends, relatives, and hitchhikers to your house on short notice.

For me, a "stay-cation" is when you put away the car keys after bringing home a stack of really great reading material, a couple of bottles of Howard Soon's syrah, and a pile of DVDs that have received high scores on metacritic.com — and then you stay PUT.

You don't go to the airport. You don't spend two grand on an enhanced oil change. You don't pack your bags. You simply stay home, sleep in, nap every few hours, and, of course, eat, read and watch like a voracious pig.

My wife believes that life is about creating great memories. Before I met her, I thought life was all about trying to avoid death, especially a painful death. This philosophy, born of reading too much French existential literature, caused me to live a life of ritual.

"Dad," says my ten-year-old son, "you mean you lived a totally boring life before you met Mom." Well, since my wife reads this column, I have to say yes. But on the other hand, I tend to really like the simple things in life.

Do you know what I mean? Instead of peak experiences designed by corporations to form the basis of our BIG-TIME vacation-style memories, I tend to derive a great deal of satisfaction from doing the same simple things over and over again.

For instance, waking up without any pain rates super high on my list. I really like staring out the window at some kind of lovely view. I also like reading the *Courier* with a nice Bean Scene latte by my side. I also love holding my children in my arms when they crawl over me because they are bored.

"Boredom is good," I whisper in their ears. Boredom is the root of creativity; it is the prelude to genius. Boredom, if you are lucky, allows you to go beyond routine and enter the realm of transcendence. Boredom can change you.

The daily rituals of home, especially when we are not on vacation, are often ignored and unappreciated. That's why the "staycation," a vacation from your vacation, can be pure glory.

The Host from Hell

Have you had them yet? I bet you have. Everybody has them. You can't avoid them. Who are these invaders? Some people call them vermin or parasites, ranging in pockets of various populations throughout the valley. We call them house guests.

If my house guests stay for less than three days, everything is great. But once the visit goes beyond three days, something happens to me. I start turning green, my breath goes sour, and I become a warped version of the Incredible Hulk, the vicious and destructive host from hell.

Normally, I'm a pretty mellow guy. I'm generous with my guests. I am not chintzy with my Nota Bene. I don't count out the prawns with an abacus, and I don't stopwatch your hot showers. I will even laugh at your jokes and stories that wouldn't be so funny if you were around more. Sure, I'm tempted to yawn but I never do. You darn house guests mean a lot to us!

Honestly, most of us put on a nice spread for our guests. We do what we can to be hospitable. I think you can tell a lot about yourself by what kind of host you are. I know people who are ridiculously unconscious hosts. They ask you to stay, but are too busy to remove the stains from their bathrooms. You have to ask them for clean sheets and towels. And around 8 p.m. you start making dinner for them be-cause they are still at work.

Hosts can be divided into two camps: the good ones and the ones from hell. The good ones anticipate what you need, pop that frosty organic beer into your hand just when you really need it, and they also know through some kind of sixth sense how to get out of your way. It's a wonderful art being a great host. You have to have empathy. At least that's what I hear.

People who are bad hosts tend to be that way for two reasons: 1) they have no idea what other people want or need; 2) they have had so many bad guests they just can't be bothered any more.

I hate to say it, but I'm not the greatest of hosts (nor am I much of a guest, but that's another story). What? You too? My friend Heather told me that she had house guests that brought their dog at treat (without permission) and the cute little mutt deposited some indel-ible gems on their new carpets. Did these guests pay for carpet clean-ing? Nope.

Sometimes house guests just expect to be served hand and foot; sometimes they miraculously jump up and cook dinner for you. Guests come in all shapes and forms. Sooner or later, especially if you live in the Okanagan, you're tempted to type up a list of rules for your guests. So here are my rules – feel free to tape to your refrigera-tor.

RULES FOR OKANAGAN HOUSEGUESTS

1. Three days makes for a perfect visit. Plenty of time to enjoy, chat, and appreciate the joys of togetherness. After three days, please go ahead and move on to a hotel or campsite. If you insist on staying longer, please be aware that we are planning to rent your room to high-paying tri-athletes in the next 24 hours.

2. Gifts are good. They are very good. Real good. Did I tell you we really appreciate gifts? Gifts are expected if you make a mess of things, break stuff, or love to talk solely about yourself. Even if you don't cause any trouble, you should at least take your host family out for dinner on the last night. If you're on a budget, offer to cook dinner. If you can't cook, surprise your host with something delight-ful. You can never have enough Riedel crystal wine glasses. I hint you not.

3. Please attempt to do your own *&%$ dishes or at least load the *&%$ dishwasher. Setting your glasses on the floor to be tripped

over is not good manners. Neither is hiding behind the newspaper when the dishes start getting cleared. Unbuckling your belt, belching the alphabet, and demanding the TV remote is the hostess's job, not yours! This rule does not count if you save the host's marriage or fix something that has been broken a long time.

4. If you stay for over a week, you must try with all your might not to fight with your partner. We hosts are so tired of providing separate rooms to warring spouses. Kiss and make up on the premises; don't wait to do it when you go home. After you've forgotten your latest dust-up, we'll still remember how you took turns slagging each other, so be nice.

5. If you borrow the host's car for more than a few hours, please return it washed and with a full tank of gas. If you burn up the brakes or a pull a honkin' horse trailer to Conkle Lake, you ought to do something appropriately respectful without being asked. The best guests do not wait to be asked to be helpful or considerate.

6. If you are a heavy drinker, then replace at least fifty percent of what you drink, especially if you're staying at a place that offers really good stuff. If you're slamming four bottles of pinot noir a night for three nights, that's like $250, even for an average pinot noir. Don't replace the good stuff with Yellowtail. Go to Quail's Gate or Cedar Creek and choose something that will be appreciated.

7. Know when to get lost. Many families need their private time every day. Sometimes families like to enjoy a few minutes of alone time at night. Try to understand this before cannon-balling into their hot tub. Young families, in particular, need a lot of time to bathe and get their young ones ready for bed. Be aware of this before suggesting that five is too early for dinner. If you really want to be the guest from heaven, offer to babysit on one of those nights. Give your hosts a treat. After all, many of us will be hosting from April to November.

8. Understand morning rituals. Everybody has one-of-a-kind morning rituals just like you do. Just because you like "beer, bran, and bathroom fan" at 5am doesn't mean that your hosts will want to

celebrate with you. Breakfast can be a sensitive time, so turn your demands into hints and requests. I am picky about the morning paper. I especially do not love reading the *Courier* when it is covered with coffee rings, egg bits, and bacon spittle.

9. Unless you're a very close relative, please don't ask us to go with you on wine tastings. We locals love our local wine, but there are only so many times a year we can go to Mission Hill without feeling like we work there. Wine-touring is a really fun activity to do WITHOUT your hosts. And when you return, no doubt showing off all your new bottles, do be so kind as to reserve one or two bottles of Oculus for your fine hosts.

10. Ask nicely to use the computer. People can get awfully picky about their computers. Do not jump onto the host's keyboard and start downloading movies from eastern Europe. If you're going to scan your favourite porn sites, it would be really smart to acquaint yourself with the Criminal Code of Canada.

My guests, unfortunately, do not receive great service after a week. No matter who you are, you're going to be irritating after a week. Even if your bathroom and kitchen manners surpass the Queen's, you'll soon start to wear out your welcome.

After a week, you will become part of the family, and at my house that means more than rent and chores. It means not expecting your personal stories to be met with delightful laughter and witty repartee; it means being a contributor and not just a receiver.

Yes, I guess I am the host from hell. Sorry, I've got a lot of room for improvement. Of course, you know you're always welcome at my pad. Really.

STAN CHUNG

Visit from Grandmother

When I was in grade five, my grandmother died. This was the mid-seventies. She came to Canada in 1972, a small but stocky sixty-year-old woman who spoke little English. She stayed with us in Williams Lake for less than a year, and then she found a second-story apartment overlooking Main Street in Vancouver.

The neon from the car dealership flashed into her apartment at night. It wasn't the greatest area, but she rode the electric buses, took care of herself, and waited for our visits. We were all very relieved she no longer lived with us.

At the age of eleven, I believed I was the only one who could understand my grandmother. The anger boiled inside her, and it didn't take much for her to start pounding the floors and walls while using the most exotic of swear words. After these episodes, I would sit in my room, wondering if I should go to her, hold her hand, and listen to her. But I did not.

"Your father is useless," she would yell. "He's supposed to be a minister, but he can't even take care of his poor mother!"

Over the years, these memories, cloudy and confused, have made me dizzy. The four year old in me wants to believe that she tried to separate me from my parents, and so I ended up eating her food and tormenting her. The revenge of a four year old. People say it is easy to forget, especially when you are young, but I wish I could remember better. The year I lived with her in Korea, after my parents had left for Canada, did something to me.

When she lived with us in Williams Lake, I treated her very poorly. I was older and felt there was nothing she could do to me.

My father, mother, sister, and I were not only afraid of her, but we talked about her behind her back. We talked about how loudly she chewed her food. We made fun of her broken English. We greeted her old-country cooking with mock horror.

I was probably the worst because I feared her so little. I was rebellious, disrespectful, and spoiled. One day she made us some delicious, soft-white buns with sweet red beans inside. It took her two days to make them. I gobbled them up greedily without appreciation. I was horrible and nobody stopped me. Finally, she decided to live in Vancouver.

(Whenever anyone came to visit us, it didn't take long for us to drive that person away. Other than saying we were awful people, I do not know why. We tore people apart with petty criticisms and resentments.)

My grandmother grew up in a small peasant village on a volcanic island between Korea and Japan. She spent most of her life under Japanese occupation. Living under occupation, as most Koreans of that generation will tell you, strengthens your identity but you pay the price because of the resentment that rots your stomach like acid. My grandmother, Bong Choon Chung was an illiterate single parent and a born-again Christian. She survived by growing vegetables and taking them to market on weekends. She was married twice. My grandfather died shortly after my father was born. The second man she married left to work in Manchuria, not long after my uncle was born.

When we heard grandmother had died, we drove in our Mercedes down to Vancouver. It was a seven-hour drive that passes through many geo-climatic zones. We passed 100 Mile House, Clinton, Yale, Chilliwack, and finally arrived in Vancouver where the air was moist and faintly smelling of cedar and ocean.

She was buried in Vancouver on a cold day. The funeral service, the first for me, was attended by Korean families throughout the lower mainland. Today, there is a huge population of Koreans, but in those days, it seemed we all knew each other. The day after we arrived, my father's half-brother, an electronics businessman from Chicago, burst into our hotel room and blustered promises to us.

"You kids. You study hard. I pay for your university. Your grandmother was murdered by bad doctor, and I make sure he pays. Tomorrow, we go shopping and I buy you anything you want."

Of course, none of these things happened. My grandmother died as a result of gall bladder surgery complications, and my uncle didn't hire or know any hit men. I don't even know where my uncle is now. I hear he is keeping a low profile in the Pacific Northwest after he scammed a large retailer out of a cheque large enough to retire on.

Korean funerals are a little different. First of all, there is the custom of envelope giving. People lined up at the hotel room and slipped my father thick envelopes. Afterwards, I saw my father count up the stacks and stacks of cash, and to me, it seemed like a scene out of a Hollywood movie.

The next day, we sat in a long white limousine and arrived at the church. I sat in a hard pew beside my little sister. My parents entered behind the casket and that's when I heard the long, low, nearly hysterical cries of my father. I had never heard that sound before and I've never heard it again. Then my mother joined in. Her cries filled the church and she collapsed. I hung my head, closed my eyes, and could not understand.

Seeing our mother cry, made my sister and I cry, too. I wondered if my grandmother was watching us. Our sadness, our sorrow, our guilt. There were so many things to cry for, but who really understood what it was like for my grandmother.

Later, we drove to the cemetery. I was amazed by the long row of cars behind us. To be the centre of attention in this way was strange. People who I didn't know, bowed to my parents and embraced them. I stood in the distance. Nobody shook my hand or clapped me on the shoulder. Finally, a relative stood beside me, and I felt better, at least someone recognized me.

On that cold November day, there were no tears for my grand-mother. I blinked hard and tried, but the wind cooled my eyes, and I kept looking up for snow. A bit of frozen rain moved diagonally as people put up their black umbrellas. There were a lot of people there, but it was very quiet. The sleet hit the ground and bounced. For a moment, I could see snow on Grouse Mountain and then the cloud cover came. There was a lot of mud around the casket, but the ground was hard. I waited for my uncle to do something hysterical, but he stood with his hands in his pockets and kept pushing up his glasses.

My parents wiped their eyes.

We never visited my grandmother's grave except maybe once, the following year, and for some reason, all I can remember is my mother putting plastic flowers next to her bronze marker.

It has been many decades now and I have not visited my grand-mother. I know her grave sits at Ocean View Cemetery, and I try not to wonder about what kind of person I was and have become. After all, I am too busy. I am a father now with young children of my own. My own parents have passed on and left us alone.

It is April, and my daughter has just turned nine. Clementine still cries when I leave town on business. She misses me. I wonder how old she will be before she stops crying. How long will she love me like this? And what, I ask myself, when I sit in that hotel room far away, have I done to deserve those beautiful tears.

I think about tears, the tears in my daughter's eyes, the tears in my own, and the frozen tears in the sky the day my grandmother was buried, and I think about how it must have been for me to lose my parents for that year while they settled in a new land. And how it must have been for my little sister who believed she'd never see her parents again. And how it must have been for my grandmother who stayed in Korea to raise us, and love us, and who is now nearly for-gotten.

Parents Gone Wild

In a culture of "under-parenting" where we employ video games, computers, and televisions to care for our children, we still manage to find fascinating and contradictory ways to parent. No longer are we either an "under-parent" or an "over-parent." We are at once two creatures: one neglectful, the other controlling.

We've all heard about the kid who has no time for unplanned creative time. Every day, the kid is rushed off to hockey or soccer, church or outdoor club, music or dance, or to a play date with a "pre-approved" classmate.

Our kids are busy eight days a week. We have the high mileage vehicles and the mounds of house clutter to prove it.

We've all heard about the over-parent who micro-manages every teacher, principal, and custodian within sight. Principals tell horror stories illustrating the bullying tactics of parents trying not only to choose teachers and classmates, but also the teachers and classmates of everybody else.

Coaches have felt the sting of parental scrutiny. All coaches know parents who fling honey or vinegar to make sure little Madison or Jeremiah receives preferred treatment.

"Life is not fair," the coach says "A little adversity never hurt anyone." But you and I both know that sometimes it's way easier just to let the parents go wild.

Will nobody stand up to us, we beastly parents from hell?

Just what happened to us anyway? What has happened to parenthood? When did it turn into a death sport? And what happens to our coddled, micro-managed kids when they hit adulthood? Where will this culture of privilege, neglect, and intimidation lead?

Under-parented kids are easy to spot. They scream in grocery stores, wear diapers under their jeans, and eat like pythons. The under-parented kid will swallow anything. They'll eat pizza cardboard as long as the cheese grease is there. A haphazard diet of Kraft dinner and pizza has made the under-parented kid a connoisseur of bad nutrition.

On the other hand, over-parented kids can fly under the radar. They are usually quiet and reserved, just like your average serial killer. Years of mom and dad picking apart your every move will turn you into a placid robot. These kids may be obedient, but inside they yearn to prove themselves worthy of the one thing you can't stop withholding: love without conditions, contracts, or unreachable standards.

When it comes to food, over-parented kids eat like royalty. Either it's their way or puke on the highway. Our kids use food to make their demands. How else to make sense of this oppressive and confusing parental love?

I know one kid who forces himself to retch and upchuck as soon as the dinner hour comes around. Hey, it's the only way he can control the agenda.

Ever heard over-parents talking to their kid? Over-parents love being right, and they relish winning their disagreements with their kids. After all, what's the use of being a powerful parental figure if you can't be pompous, patronizing, and condescending?

When not providing corrective lectures, we parents can be oh, so generous. We cruise the aisles buying useless junk for our kids: remorse through credit card. In the check out line, we call it love and lord it over them.

"I bought this $60 video game for you," we say "Now quit your whining, show me some gratitude, and stop looking at me with that clown face and sad eyes."

My parents never walked me to school, picked me up from anything, or badgered the principal about my bullies. I not only ate what was on my plate, but I licked it clean. I know they worried about me, but they rarely intruded or advocated for me. And sometimes I wish they did.

Today's parents realize that we are the sole provider for our children. We know that if we do not push the agenda forward, nobody else will. When I taught university English classes, I knew that many of the papers I marked were co-written by well-meaning over-parents.

I remember one kid with a beard and baby face who came into my office and said, "My mom worked really hard on this essay, sir, and she would like to know how we can improve the grade. You really don't want her coming in, do you?"

Parents have a lot at stake when it comes to our kids. Their success is ours. We want our little heroes to taste glory. We want what's best for them, but we also know who is really holding them back.

When we worry about their popularity, we deny that popularity may be our own childhood issue. When we force martial arts or ballet upon them, we may be denying our own violent and ungraceful histories. When we tell them that academic achievement doesn't count, we may be betraying our own disappointments.

If we are not careful, they will become us.

It's not easy being a parent. We face awful pressures. The worst pressure of all comes from our own parents. Just like our parents before us, we bestow our personality flaws to our offspring in exaggerated and magnified ways. Parenthood: it's the gift that keeps on giving and giving.

Whatever our flaws as human beings, what we should strive to remember is the true purpose of parenthood: to foster a balanced journey toward independence.

Whenever I control or neglect, nag or bite my tongue, I ask myself if I am nurturing independence. Am I helping my child grow up or am I holding my child back? Are they doing it for them or me?

GLOBAL CITIZEN

We love our children, despite all they learn from us. And no matter what we do, no matter how we parent, our children grow up a little bit every day. Let's hope that we parents do the same.

On Transformation

Do you have a favourite coach or teacher? Has anyone ever positively impacted your life in a way that stays with you forever? A great teacher, a superb administrator, a wonderful boss, a caring parent — all these roles have the potential to transform.

I tend to see three levels of learning: transmission, transaction, and transformation. It's easy to understand how knowledge is transmitted from teacher to learner. Students memorize the textbook, whip out the highlighter, endure tests — here, knowledge gets "transmitted" from teacher to learner. Sound familiar? Actually, doing a good job transmitting knowledge is very challenging. Ask any good calculus teacher.

In most classrooms today, we expect to see interaction. Students learn from other students, and they're invited to participate in collaborative activities. When it's done really well, the student's own experiences become part of the knowledge constructed in the class. Here, learning becomes "transactional." You give: you get. Students enjoy this kind of learning because they always have something to share: themselves.

So what about "transformational" learning?

One day my son or daughter is going to tell me, "Dad, I respect you, but you're dead wrong. I don't have to believe what you believe." One view of transformational learning is that it's about critically reflecting on one's previously hidden assumptions, beliefs, and biases. Instead of turning into the Incredible Hulk, I hope I'll have the sense to recognize his/her questioning as transformational. It's about shaking your foundations (and mine). Isn't this how we grow as human beings?

Another way of looking at transformational learning is seeing it as a shift in consciousness. You see yourself, your relationships, and your principles anew. For some reason, you don't just feel it in your head; you feel it in your body, in your emotions. You say to yourself, "I am different now." This kind of learning can border on spiritual experience. That's why we teachers and learners sometimes call it an "epiphany" when we are so impacted that we feel reborn. A "good" education system develops learners with community-validated values, assumptions, and paradigms. On the other hand, a "great" education system is quite different. A great system always questions itself. It continually interrogates its deeply held values. That's why a "great" system can sometimes look like it is in continual conflict.

Asking tough questions is often met with surprise and sometimes outrage. It's quite natural to defend what we think and believe. And sometimes, we feel personally attacked. We question the strength of a relationship when we are challenged. However, it's the mark of an educated person to be courageous and open-minded enough to challenge even the deepest and most cherished of assumptions.

The history of human knowledge is filled with people and institutions of courage. Our history is also littered with people who found challenging long-held beliefs very difficult. The ideal result, of course, is a system of governance, a set of balanced laws and rights that respects social justice and the individual's rights. Believe it or not, conflict is good, so long as we have the tools, skills, and system to support dialogue and justice.

One of the greatest aspects of transformational learning is that it sets you free. Through the help of a great teacher, you reach a point of epiphany. Epiphany is that moment in your life when you see the light, when you finally put it together, when you finally see yourself and your place in the world.

To be enlightened this way sometimes requires a wonderful teacher, mentor, or guide. When was the last time you achieved a moment of epiphany? What did you learn about yourself? How did it change your life? And if you're a teacher, how well do you understand the structure of epiphany?

When I look back upon my life and recall my favourite teachers, I realize that my greatest teacher was my father. When I was a teenager, my father and I spent a lot of time in conflict. In my twenties, he even challenged my decision to be a teacher.

"Son, why do you want to teach? Is it because you know better?"

"I want to help people, Dad," I replied somewhat defensively.

"Why? Do you want to help people for you or for them? Why do you want to help people?"

At that moment, I realized that those in helping roles possess enormous responsibilities. If you do it to feed your ego, to make yourself feel valued, or to satisfy a need for power, then you really have to ask yourself the question my father asked me: "Why do you want to help people?"

I've never forgotten the lesson he taught me that day. Decades later, I have become acutely aware of my feelings when I am confronted with someone who needs my help. I ask myself how my feelings impact my role as a helper. If you want to be that transformational teacher, mentor, coach, or parent, then one of the first things you need to do is understand your emotional responses to those you want to help.

I respect all those people who choose to help others. Whether, you're coaching hockey, listening to a friend's problems, or being a supportive grandparent, there is nothing more important than watching someone succeed in making a meaningful transformation. But in the end, we must be vigilant about our own feelings, ego needs, and desire for power.

I have met people who needed my help, but who I had to turn away. I have met others who I felt were toxic to me, and I had to learn to create firm boundaries in order to help them. I had to do these things because I recognized emotions in myself that I knew would cause me trouble. I've also faced others who thought I was an incredible genius, and I had to control my ego from over-inflating and floating away!

Helping someone is a great honour and an even greater responsibility. Thanks to you and all of those who volunteer, coach, teach, and lead. And thanks to you, Dad. You taught me a lot.

This Land is Your Land

The sun never rises here. The wind howls. Thunder claps. Where the heck are we? Few dare visit this land. There is something deeply wrong. No travel guidebooks mention it.

This dark place will never be discussed at dinner. We are better acquainted with the moon even though you have been there and go there several times a week. I guarantee that you do not own a photograph of this location. No, you don't want to do business there.

I bet some of you know this place all too well. Some consider it foul, sexual, and forbidden. I wish I could stop thinking about this place, but it is a critical outlet, a final destination.

To speak of this place only serves to remind us that we are animals, creatures locked in a biological reality that joins us to every living thing on this planet.Have you figured it out yet? This great unspoken place is the dark locale we call the colon.

The colon is the great undiscovered country. It is more important to our happiness than the secrets of the ocean or the light of distant stars. This region tells us, more than any other place, who we are and how are we are doing.

Some experts suggest that this place offers us the most accurate gauge of how long we have to live. Ask any physician or physicist: what goes in must come out. And what's been coming out? Not much good, some say. Flaps of skin, say others. Whether a violent soup or a storm of stones, few of us know what to do.

Hemorrhoids, constipation, diarrhea, flatulence, irritable bowels, gas, bloating, acid reflux – the list goes on and on. One thing is indisputable: things are not right in the land down under. And most of us suffer in silence, except the ones who could generate wind power with their outbursts.

Some physicians say that two, three, even four snake-like, greenish-brown bowel movements daily are an excellent measure of your gastrointestinal and digestive health. In short, your stools are your report card. And in this respect most of us are C students. C, if you didn't know, is for constipation. I admit to the massive numbers reading this that I have been a C student off and on since the late eighties.

Constipation is no joking matter, say the experts. Constipation is serious crap. Constipation tells me that I'm not eating well, that I'm not digesting my food properly, that I am risking my longterm health. Constipation of the body, moreover, suggests constipation of the mind. Our lives of rush, stress, and inactivity do not allow us to reflect on how things are coming out. I must admit that my movements haven't been wonderful lately. They do not slither. They do not coil to the left in the curve of the small intestine. So what? Who cares? Well, we are talking about a problem regarded as the most common medical complaint in North America.

Moreover, how can we think and act properly when a majority of us suffer down below? How can we take care of our loved ones when we ourselves are functioning at less than our potential? How can I be a good parent if I raise children who are also constipated by the indiscriminate swallowing of food-like substances that possess little redeeming nutritional value and serve best to cause intestinal traffic jams, anal gridlock, and foul, acidic, head-on collisions with white porcelain.

I am constipated, and I'm not going to take it anymore!

People talk about global warming and want to know what they can do to become global citizens. I say, how do you expect to change the world if you spend half your time and energy worrying about your next dump? How do you put in a full day's passion and energy if your hemmoroids are killing you?

My digestive health begins with a focus on fibre. I've started reading labels and checking grams of fibre per serving. I want to eat at least 35 grams of fibre a day. I'm eating one colour a lot – brown bran for breakfast, brown bread for lunch, and brown pasta for dinner. Another thing I'm doing, and I know this sounds ridiculous, is that I'm taking the time to really chew my food, to taste it and grind it all up deliberately. Normally, I eat like a vacuum cleaner. No wonder there is heartburn, gas, bloating, and burping like there is no tomorrow. If I keep this up, will there be a tomorrow?

You have to really live in the moment to benefit from your food. This means focusing intensely on the act of tasting, chewing, and swallowing. It means sitting down, bowing your head, turning off the music, laptop, television, and chatter. I'm not up to three orchestral movements a day, but I am improving. I know you probably want me to give you a detailed update, so I am documenting my progress in a large coffee table book of detailed colour photographs to be released next holiday season. Changing the colour to greenish-brown is no easy task either. It begins with more vegetables and spinach salads. It has also meant juicing, trips down the organic aisle, and fewer coffees. Apparently caffeine gives your stools diamond-cutting powers. So much for Fair Trade. I am feeling more comfortable now. In fact, I am seriously considering a change of career: to Ace Stool Detective. Anybody can study at home to be a poop detective.

Black could mean gastritis. Maroon means see your doctor. So does gray. Beige is not good. Red could mean the dreaded hemmies have returned. Orange could mean carrots or sweet potatoes. Floaties, stinkies, white specks, black specks, mucous-coated – these all mean something to the aspiring ace stool detective.

My visits to this land have resulted in some immediate changes. I am more relaxed. I feel better, stronger, and ready to save the world.

The sun may not shine in the land down under. The wind may howl something fierce. The thunder will strike. But when everything comes out good, life is good, too.

Why I Can't Stop Trying to Smell the World

I've got a butt-ugly nose. It's broad, kind of wide, and my nostrils resemble the entrance to the Chunnel. Unfortunately, these days my *Chunn*el hasn't been working that great.

Others report big-time shnoz malfunctions as well. I know a guy who can't stop smelling his fingers. He thinks nobody is watching, but he just can't help it. This guy is clearly addicted. Every time he snorts a digit, I think of that dog sniffing your crotch or that wine snob sniffing the cork, or my dad sitting in the basement writing sermons.

Huh? What does my dad have to do with crotch-nuzzling dogs and serial finger snorters? Well, some people have NODAR, nose radar. My dad could smell anything. He was a bloodhound. I'm sure he could have had a career digging people out of avalanches or earthquakes.

When I was a kid, I'd walk into the house after school and he'd yell at me from his office: "Take your shoes off; you stepped in something!" And sure enough, I'd flip my shoe and spot a little treat, a steaming, dog bonanza brought to me by Fido and Purina.

Speaking of crap detectors, the great novelist and Nobel laureate Saul Bellow often creates heroes with supersonic noses. One character thinks he can tell how well others have wiped their bums after the toilet. How's that for a nose? Or is that maybe too much nose?

Well, the sharper your smelling instrument, the better your ability to detect the fragrance of a bruised sprig of rosemary, the wide open freshness after a summer rain, and the smell of your child's newly-washed hair. A well-functioning nose is a beautiful thing.

How about you? How do you smell? I know I am not doing well in the department of tang. I know this because my kids still have NODAR. They couldn't set foot in the new part of the mall because they couldn't stand the chemical off-gassing of the new paint and carpet. I thought it smelled like peaches.

I have to confess: I don't need to dip my fingers into my armpits, blow into my cupped hand, or take long, slow, sultry showers, covered in creamy strawberry gel. Why? I can't even smell me anymore! If forced to choose, if you really must know, I kind of smell like pork, the deep-fried sweet and sour kind. But I can't be sure.

Who will come to the rescue of our dilapidated noses? My nose is pretty much busted. I can't smell the roses or the plywood plant. My smelling powers are fading. The only thing I can do is find some way to rejuvenate my ability to breathe in, sniff, smell, and inhale. But should I even bother bringing my nose in for a refresher?

Seriously, who actually needs to smell anymore? The ultra fragrant laundry detergent and its pals Downy and Snuggle have already fried my nose, let alone triggered allergies and gastrointestinal irritation. Hey, I'm proud to say I no longer sneeze in the produce section; in the words of Carole Bayer Sager, that's what friends are for.

Herbicide and pesticide – they are old friends. I should have bought stock in chemical giants Dow and Monsanto a time ago. People talk about the dangers of second-hand cigarette smoke, but we forget about all the other stuff tickling the nose hairs (like all those cancer-evoking derivatives of Agent Orange and 2,4-D that people splatter on their gardens and lawns).

No problem, I say!

Go ahead and spray all the trees and plants with noxious chemicals. Paint my fruits and vegetables with dioxins. Dust the planet with fine particulate from my car exhaust. Who cares? I won't be able to smell it. My nose will be in retirement.

So what if food doesn't taste as it should? Even though my nose blows, I still have the crude capability to recognize that my wife's tomatoes taste about 1.8 million times better than the kind in the grocery store. Organic, free-range eggs are a delight to me; they simply rock my tired taste buds. Talk to an old-timer – bread, broccoli, beer – it doesn't taste like it used to.

The systematic, global, desensitization of our basic human senses is a tragedy. Because we can't taste, smell, see, feel, or hear anymore, we settle for crap. Not only because we can't tell the difference, but once you stop remembering how things should be, you immediately settle for a cheaper substitute. And our tastebuds aren't exactly improving: have you tasted a fast food, french fry lately? Do we really need our potatoes coated with exclusive chemicals and fried twice? Some used to aspire getting off the power grid; now we wonder if we need off the industrialized food grid.

You are what you eat. Your brain functions on the nutrients you provide. Basically, you think what you eat. My daughter clucks. Why, oh why, did I raise her on McNuggets? My son moos. Kill me now. Take me to daddy jail.

If we teach our children to taste and smell and see, maybe they will put a stop to what we have done. We stopped smelling the air and proceeded to stink it up. We stopped drinking out of our taps, so we settle for plasticized water. We stopped protecting the ecosystem, so now we go to zoos to visit our jailed animal friends.

We did not think because we could not feel.

But we do have a chance, especially if we use educated feelings to consume. Our consumption rules the world. If you buy a car with your ears, you will understand that cars have not changed at all in fifty years. At 120 km/hr, it's at least 70 db of white noise no matter what the brand. If you buy a product with your feelings, you'll ask yourself why does this smell, feel, taste, and sound this way? Does a clean house mean you plug in some chemically-derived fragrance to spray the air every fifteen minutes?

For car makers, home builders, and product designers smell is the new frontier. Our sense of smell is strongly linked to our emotions. Mercedes is patenting their new car smell. We human beings are so stupid we now want our cars to smell like chemical off-gassing. Yum. The upper class wants leather and walnut. Jaguar has already added these chemical fragrances to their cars and turbocharged sales. It's the all-new scratch and sniff.

When one person's perfume is another person's poison, we know we're up the creek. What are you smelling right now? A carpet teeming with microscopic mold spores? An oven cleaner decorated with poison signs? A fat steak laced with synthetic hormones? Your own body odour derived from a diet consisting of endocrine disrupting substances?

I hope my grandchildren will not miss what it truly feels like to be alive; I hope they will taste the briskness of cool mountain air and experience walking through an old growth forest. Go outside and take a deep breath. What do you smell? Do you detect that faint fragrant scent in the distance? Breathe again. What is that smell? It's our robust, beautiful and dying planet offering us hope.

Why I Can't Stop Thinking about Cars

I am afraid of snakes. Vampire bats, too. I do not love reptiles or sharks of any sort. I especially loathe the kind of beast that can snap off your leg and suck on the joint like you might slurp a hot wing at KFC.

In the total scheme of things reptiles are not that bad, even the human kind with wrinkly necks who smell like baby powder whom you call grandma. Nope, I love seniors, even the ones who stop at green lights. They deserve our every courtesy because one day, if we are lucky, our legs will resemble ostrich skin, and you will complain that my corduroys emanate.

We all fear aging, but it's not really the killer we make it out to be. We know all about the subject, so through the years we count the inevitable sequence of steps: birth, kindergarten, high school, creaking joints, children, reading glasses, faulty memory, and I forget the rest. In elementary school, I remember jumping off roofs, skateboarding behind buses, and eating partially-cooked hamburger. Nothing happened to me. In high school, I did worse, and they rewarded me with a driver's license.

Just in case you didn't know, driving is the real killer. If you can safely avoid automobiles, you're going to live a long time. You know the stats: more people are killed or injured driving than practically anything else. But that doesn't stop us from saying, "Hey, kids, instead of swimming with piranhas or playing with matches, let's go for a drive!"

Aren't automobiles wonderful? The rain-sensing wipers on my friend Charlotte's BMW will save you the energy-robbing chore of matching your wiper speed to the volume of rain. We're only years away from that Korean-made sedan with the leather seats, 17 air bags, 48 speakers, and turbo-charged hybrid engine with 500 horsepower that will take two teaspoons of gas. All that with zero-percent interest over twenty years.

If you watch television, you have been programmed to love new cars. If you grew up in the fifties, you lived in an era of the open highway, drive-in movie, and slippery back seat. If you grew up in the sixties and seventies, muscle cars with rumbling exhausts make you fondly recall burn-outs in front of the junior high, midnight cruises at 80 mph, and smoky bush parties. If you grew up the eighties or nineties, cars represent responsibility, adulthood, freedom. Ask anyone of any age, there is nothing quite as beautiful as a nice set of mags.

Every generation has a crop of automobiles that set the cultural standard. This branding was achieved through television and movie advertising that made sure our sense of luxury, our sense of rebellion, our sense of life itself, was somehow wrapped up with the automobile. Just think about what James Bond and James Dean did for Aston Martins and Porsches. What Herbie and Steve McQueen did for the Beetle and the Mustang. Look at what recent video games and movies have done for the Honda Civic, known as the archetypal tuner car.

Our culture tells us that you are what you drive. Or more accurately, you drive what you want to be. You can be just like the Ferrari driven by the hero of Miami Vice – cool, refined, unsocked. You, too, can be that sleek, silver Odyssey with your love of soccer, lingerie, Disney movies, and Lululemon. You are that beat-up '86 Tempo. You work long and hard to pay for your 60-inch Toshiba, basement suite, and Ramen noodle diet. You are that Mercedes Smart car because you are enlightened, retired, and cashmere-wearing. Brands have reached a subconscious ability to define who we are and who we want to be. And all we want to be is our true selves, right?

Whether you drive Camry, Camero or Cayman, the mighty car is our greatest joy, second most expensive possession, and the suffocation of this planet. A world without automobiles is nearly impossible to imagine. Only a skilled science fiction writer can conjure a world without exhaust. Imagine what our communities would look like if they were not bisected by roads, avenues, and superhighways. Imagine all the space taken up by hot asphalt parking lots suddenly gone. What would we build in their place?

What would you do if you could not drive? Where else would you have those heart to hearts? What would happen if gas prices suddenly tripled? Would we take a horse and cart downtown for sushi and latte? Or would we paddle our kids to morning hockey practice on a Venice-like canal system? Would Westsiders complain about the sway of the cable tram that would carry them in their suits and folding bicycles across Lake Okanagan? How many relatives and friends would irritate us with their vitality because they have been unpestered and unmaimed and unkilled by traffic?

Just how unbearable would life be without the automobile?

We'd probably ride bicycles. Would there be a significant product range of bicycle doggy baskets? Would bicycles come standard with air bags, anti-lock brakes, and air-conditioning? Would families pull their children around in bike trailers outfitted with DVD players and LCD screens? Would teens pedal around in customized bikes loaded with bass-thumping, Eminem-blaring stereos? What would the squeegee people do?

Without cars would we become a community of walkers, strollers, and midnight stalkers? Would we wear our walking shoes in style, become obsessed with comfort footwear, performance footwear, all-terrain footwear? Would we delight in the non-materialistic splendor of going barefoot? Would our television screens be flooded with shoe ads, sock ads, and foot powder ads? Would feet become sexy? Would you be unable to pull your eyes away from her big toe cleavage? Augmented? Probably.

Wouldn't our homes look different? What would we do with these gigantic monstrosities formerly known as garages? Wouldn't they disappear along with roads and sidewalks and cul-de-sacs? Our houses would take on other forms. Think of Kettle Valley without the asphalt. (Would anyone live that far out of town?) Our homes would probably be dominated by the front porch and not the double garage. People would no longer drive into their homes and disappear. Conversations between neighbours would spring up all over, just like the plants and greenery busting cracks through asphalt. How long would it take the green, green grass of home to cover the gray, gray glory of our petrochemical past?

What harm has the automobile caused? Plenty. Cars have changed our lives in so many ways. We love them for their speed and beauty, but we've also been taught to worship them as idols, to ignore what damage they have done to our communities, and to think there can be no life without them.

The cult known as car worship will not be broken in this generation or next. Hollywood stars like George Clooney may encourage us to drive electric cars and take public transit, but that will not change our addiction. Our love of transportation can be replaced by other forms of cruising. In Holland, they have created a set of strategies to promote the bicycle and calm the traffic. Traffic calming is a lot more than setting up speed bumps. You can achieve it by narrowing the roads, changing their elevation, and creating an environment where pedestrians are more important than traffic. If we can't stop driving, maybe we can drive less and drive slower.

I am afraid of snakes. I am afraid of growing old. But most of all, I am afraid of my life being cut short by a traffic accident. It takes a split second of inattention for someone to plow through an intersection and nail you. It takes one tiny section of black ice to change your life and the lives of loved ones forever. Slow down. Give yourself a fighting chance to chase your grandchildren, to walk barefoot with the one you love. Give yourself a chance to grow old.

When the Going Gets Tough

"Thirty-three countries around the world face potential social unrest because of the acute hike in food and energy prices."
— ROBERT ZOELICK, *President, World Bank*

The global economic crisis is more than a crisis. It is a test of our basic assumptions about how we want to live. In a way, this crisis is also a political one: it may signal the impotency of the American lifestyle. It may also be a spiritual crisis: a time when we ask ourselves what truly matters.

Instead of seizing this opportunity for critical reflection, many continue to espouse the idea that we can shop our way out of this mess. When the going gets tough, they reason, the tough go shopping. Here is the flawed logic: in order to resolve our cycle of debt, let us pile on some more. Instead of aligning our economy with a new vision of how we want to live, there is a strong argument that all we need to do is turn back the clock.

To believe that renewed consumption is the answer to this crisis reflects a blindness to the fact that our lifestyle, especially in the last twenty years of excess, has essentially backfired upon us. Only the truly addicted can argue that the answer to the problem of our debt and over-consumption is to continue to do more of the same. On the contrary, this is an opportunity to align our values, make strategic choices, and invest in ourselves.

What kind of world do you want to live in? We all realize that excess has harmed our planet, created huge inequities, and propelled selfishness above collaboration. Selfishness is antithetical to our political ideology: democracy. If democracy is about anything, it is about sharing: sharing our ideals, sharing our resources, sharing our belief that together we are much better off than as individuals.

The water in our pipes, the streets in front of our homes, the rule of law in our courts, the work of nurses, teachers, and social workers — to name but a few — are all a result of our collective strength as citizens of this democratic country. But our collective strength is threatened by this crisis in ways that conventional investments in physical infrastructure, tax cuts, and industry loans do not address.

Listen carefully, this economic crisis brings with it the potential for unprecedented social unrest. When things get tough, people just don't buy freezers; they buy into fear and insecurity.

We will watch things get worse, some of us will become victims, and we will decide out of fear to invest in prisons, security systems, and selfishness. The unreported story of 2009 is that social chaos is brewing in the United States and throughout the world; there is too much social and economic inequity built upon capitalism gone wild. The poor despise the rich. The rich see no reason to share. Handgun purchases went up 39% in Obama's home state of Illinois in November 2008. When capitalism and democracy go head to head, who wins?

What does history tell us happens when people lose jobs, houses, and dignity? The first thing we do is look for scapegoats; our first temptation is to protect what we have and lock out those who might make us afraid. Ask any religious or spiritual leader, crisis teaches how much or little our values mean to us.

What will you do when times get tough? Who will you turn to? Who will you blame? What will be your first investment? Will you invest in video surveillance or upgrade your education? Will you insist upon slashing social programs or demand an improvement in this province's dismal child poverty? Will you support early childhood learning or electrify your fence?

Instead of turning our backs on those who are the victims of this crisis, we must believe in the principle that we are defined by how we treat our most vulnerable. Instead of just investing in public infrastructure, let us invest in social infrastructure.

What is our social infrastructure? Our schools, our hospitals, our legal system, our system of welfare and employment insurance —like it or not, the quality of these public institutions forms the backbone of what makes Canada unique, special, and yes, not as vulnerable to crisis as other nations.

Our public health system, once seen by Americans as Canada's unfair subsidy, is now seen correctly for what it is: an enormous competitive advantage for this nation. Our health care and education system have attracted newcomers for decades. Our literacy rates and post-secondary participation rates are the envy of the world. Our justice system and our social safety net provide all of us with the basic rights and freedoms of a leading democratic society. Most of the world possesses systems that are corrupt, unreliable, and dominated by the privileged. Why not invest in our social infrastructure? Why not invest in extending Canada's competitive advantage?

Entrepreneurs and businesses want lower taxes, but only a fool would want to erode Canada's enviable health, education, legal, and social safety net. If we erode our health care system, the private sector will bear the costs, and we have all seen what happened to General Motors without a national health plan. Where would the American worker and the American corporation be today if Americans had a public health insurance plan ten years ago?

If we invest our resources and efforts wisely, we might avoid much suffering. But at the same time, we need to face the need for a new vision for Canada. We need to agree on what we should be investing in. We need to enhance our policy development infrastructure and enact laws to create incentives that support our values as well as invigorate social and physical infrastructure investment. While we're at it, it's time to reconfigure our tax system. Let's tax consumption, not income.

What else do we need?

Policy, policy, policy. It was boring old policy that inoculated our banking industry. It will be boring old policy that rescues us. In terms of energy, we need to make investments in how energy is delivered across vast distances. We need more citizen-ownership of our energy sources so that our children can – one fine day – utilize clean and independent energy.

In terms of health policy, we need to focus on addressing our sedentary, TV-based, lifestyle. We need better places to walk, play, and congregate. We need to get to work and school using innovative forms of public transportation. We need to improve how we move people and how we move goods. In Germany, condominium owners are teaming together to purchase six cars, for example, to be shared by all units, so that no one person needs to maintain the expense.

In some European cities, streetcars transport goods to shops and warehouses. In São Paulo, outdoor advertising may become illegal. Isn't it time to reduce the subsidy on marketing expenditures? Let's free our eyeballs from the visual pollution of global marketing and reclaim the beauty of our public spaces. It's amazing what happens when you share your values and your possessions: you become closer to your neighbours, you benefit from the bounty of many gardens, and you begin realizing that selfishness is wasteful and needlessly expensive.

In other words, you plant seeds.

We need our universities and colleges to focus their research on areas that align with our public policy priorities. We are a small country; we don't have the resources to be all things to all people. We can focus our cancer research, for example, on early detection. Policy experts tell us we will save lives this way. We need to better support the parents of every newborn, so that Canada's child never knows what it feels like to be harmed or go without proper nutrition. We need to price unhealthy foods and activities to match their costs on our health care system.

We need to catch people before they fall.

We need to make sure everyone who starts an enterprise has a chance to compete in a fair, not free, marketplace. We need a program to bring Canadians closer together, so we can renew our collective sense of optimism, strengthen our ability to withstand any crisis, and educate the world on what it means to invest in ourselves.

The crisis is near. No country will be untouched. No family will be without suffering. But we can prevail. If we reflect on our values and invest in our social infrastructure, a strengthened Canada will emerge.

Life a la carte

I marvel at people who walk the beach with metal detectors. They sway their wands, awaiting the next gleaming washer or diamond earring. These "ground anglers" pursue the prized lunker, not knowing if the beeping signifies monster or minnow. I'm sure it's a fine hobby; probably better for you than bingo dabbing or lottery scratching, both fine pursuits requiring money and astronomical luck.

Like these fishers of sand, most people can't resist the urge to collect. One friend collects beautiful Persian carpets. Others find delight in crystal figurines. It used to be either stamps or coins, but today, after decades of human rights struggles, you're allowed to collect pretty much anything.

And we do.

I happen to collect paper, mainly bills and invoices. I have been doing it involuntarily for years. As a matter of fact, I have bills that go back decades. I keep them in yellow envelopes and boxes from the liquor store. Will old unpaid invoices be seriously collected one day on eBay? To go with my middle-class collection of bills, I have a middle-class side-hobby: collecting money-saving tips.

Whenever I am near an A&W, duck pond, or scooter store, I like to talk with someone from a previous generation. I do this because I want to add to my collection of money-saving tips.

My esteemed elders warn that saving money is an art. It is tough and surprisingly dangerous work. You may not achieve much success at the beginning. You will be shunned by our culture, especially by those who can't resist the temporarily soul-fulfilling act of letting money slip through the fingers. The professional savers among us, those who live wonderfully but frugally, devote much time to the discipline. And even among the greatest of spendthrifts there arises serious risk of stupidity. Many in their effort to secure Free Stuff, Cheap Stuff, and Stuff Nobody Wants That You Can Sell for a Hell of a Lot, have fallen by the wayside and ended up pushing a wobbly Safeway cart into the bush.

So before we get to Life a la carte, the ultimate in penny-pinching, let's start with a few basics. One of the first rules of saving money is to pack all your spending into one day a week. Spend money on Saturdays or Wednesdays, and for the rest of the week sit on your purse or wallet. Try this and you'll discover that a day can't go by without you wanting to throw away money. I know true artists that can go weeks without spending mindlessly. They buy enough wholesome food to last the duration. They grind, brew, and drink their own coffee. They read other people's newspapers and use the library. They attend free cultural events put on by the city with their tax dollars. They make lovely sandwiches to take to work. They use their teabags twice. In the past, those days before Interac, these people were known as Mr. and Mrs. Normal.

We spend about a thousand dollars a month on food. I find this a ridiculous amount. My parents survived on much less. And my grandparents ate only rice on Tuesdays. I tell my children that they don't need breakfast, Nike shoes, or clean hair. I tell my wife that we should drink powdered skim milk, grow crops, and weave our own designer fashions. And I tell myself that I can do without lattes, all-you-can-eat dim sum, and insurance of all kinds. What do families without a thousand dollars a month do for food? What would I do?

I know a penny pincher who made a decent living attending garage sales and flea markets. Everything he owns is second-hand, except I believe his underwear. He sees great environmental gains to be made by recycling. Anybody who buys a new car will tell you: as soon you drive off the lot, your car loses $3-5K in value. We pay a great price for the lovely chemical smell of the New. Garage sale folks, unfortunately, can easily go off the deep end, too, eventually renting storage to manage their excess or allowing their homes to become living and breathing junkyards. My friend has since given up on garage sales; he's gone back to being a teacher, a group of people who know a lot about penny-pitching.

Many of the teachers I know and love dress cheaply. The students require them to be dressed, not dressed well, so teachers can save a great deal by wearing clothing bought at the largest corporation in the world, Walmart. Through their donations, teachers are single-handedly helping China rise to its feet and become a dominant power. It will only be a short time before a Chinese teacher can go to Walmart in his home town and buy some underpants stitched up by a retired Canadian teacher trying to make ends meet. Thrifty is not only good for your pocketbook, but you get to play global economic politics. Just who benefits when *you* buy?

Mr. Mister, a collection agent, says that one of the best ways to stay thrifty is to collect your bills and not pay them. Surely, there are those who enjoy this sport. You collect your bills and decide in a fun game of roulette which one you're going to pay and which one you'll save for later.

How else can you afford to live in this supernatural province?

If you're really good, you get to collect all these really neat and unique collection letters such as my favourite: Pay Your Bill or We'll Turn Your Damn Heat Off. A rare bill that I'm thinking about collecting reads like this: Sell Your House or We'll Sell It For You to Collect on Your Bloody Unpaid Mortgage. Lucky recipients of that bill should know what I'm talking about it. In the eighties, it was indeed better to be foreclosed on than pay a mortgage that was worth more than your house. For those of us who don't want to collect such a bill, I suggest one simple but impossible strategy: STOP LIVING ABOVE YOUR MEANS.

The idea that you should live below your means is a pretty old-fashioned and some would say out-dated concept. Why would you want to live below your means when you have all this glorious credit to play with? Some of the penny pinchers among us feel the rest of us have been manipulated and hoodwinked. By whom you ask? By the rest of us, of course.

For example, a true penny pincher would never own a cell phone. But the rest of us say a cell phone is a necessity. The more tied down you are to someone's call, the more you are essentially a modern slave, don't you know? Penny pinchers consider their freedom to be the ultimate luxury, so being tied to the custom ring of a sexy cell phone or the beautiful fake wooden dash of that luxury SUV, is being POMP, Prisoner Of the Monthly Payment. Do you ever dream of freedom from POMP? Old-timers kindly suggest that anytime you want something that has a monthly payment attached to it, find a sock, put a ball bearing in it, and hit yourself upside the head and then maybe between your legs.

The best of the pinchers never buy the things the rest of us buy. The best have avoided collecting these former must-haves: Discman, Leatherman, George Foreman grills, ab devices, sauna suits, National Geographic, Reader's Digest, Funk and Wagnalls, indoor water fountains, indoor trampolines, indoor air fresheners, Dolby prologic, Pentium 133, microwaves, Crocs, generators, bread machines, karaoke machines, massage machines, putters, scrap-booking supplies, crystals, anything bought from TV, rock tumblers, toe socks, and tools pushed in the month of December.

Spending your hard-earned, after-tax dollars isn't easy, so it's no wonder that we sometimes give in to the strain of it all. Who doesn't need the Bee Gee's greatest hits, blonde highlights, slide-out entertainment room for your motor home, $90 dental thong, or vibrating leather furniture with cup-holders? We need this stuff, right? Would it kill us not to buy this stuff?

I guess we simply can't live without convenience. We need someone to wash, bag, and pluck our spinach for us. We need someone to put food into trays for the nutrient-robbing microwave. Some microwave products have failed in the marketplace because they require flipping after thirty seconds. You don't have time or energy to flip your microwave dinner?

While we, the middle-class, live barely one paycheque away from poverty, we do not seem willing to forego our dinners out, golf club memberships, cigarette boats, and dashes to Disneyland. I'm too tired to think about this stuff, as I recline in my remote-controlled 200-channel-plasma den of denial.

I want to tell myself that we, the middle-class, are broke, stressed, over-extended, over-pampered, and in need of working the night shift at a big-box store to pay for our necessities. Some of us middle-class, because of ill-health, family emergency, or hardluck, have been forced to miss a few payments and then find ourselves sleeping in our cars or campers. Next thing you know, we find ourselves unable to drag ourselves out of bed, and we begin disappointing the people we love. Soon, we can't help but wonder why we force ourselves to run the treadmill at work, where we toil and toil only to end up spending more than we make.

And then we wind up forced to sell our stuff and begin our careers in recycling. And we find escape in drugs, in crime, and in the simplicity of an outdoor life. I guess you could call it being homeless, Life a la carte.

To pretend not to care about the homeless is akin to caring nothing about your neighbour who may be even more over his head than you. Ask any homeless person how it feels to live without mortgage, car payment, and regular baths. It feels horrible, but at least you're free of the crushing weight of a culture that seems out of control in its obsession with things – Things You Need to Buy, Things You Need to Live, and Things You Need in Order to Feel Like You Belong.

To resist materialism seems impossible. But to do so, especially in December, may mean the difference between one way of life and another.

On Creativity

"Every act of creation is first of all an act of destruction."
— PABLO PICASSO

We have moved so many times that there are boxes that I have yet to open. These darn boxes just get moved from house to house. I recently opened one of these boxes, and I found something that I didn't quite expect: my father's writing journal.

My father died a few years ago, and I must have packed up the blue cloth binder along with all those things I couldn't bear to throw away: boxes of sermons, manual typewriter, and theology books. This particular journal begins exactly twenty years ago in the summer of 1988.

In one poem he writes about me:

This is a poem about my son Stan.
Whom I have hurt a thousand
times ...

My father began the journal when he was fifty-seven years old. He had tried to find another position as a United Church minister, but no church said yes. My parents lived in a one-bedroom condominium in Metrotown. He spent his days pursuing writing, driving my mother to and from work, and feeling lonely and useless.

He rarely shared much of his inner life with me, so his journal is a revelation. The words tell me a great deal about his despair, isolation, and fears. The journal also tells me a great deal about myself, too, because in many ways my father's struggles are my own.

The sky may be blue, the water sparkling, and the sun warm, but there are many, like my father, who have difficulty escaping their darker emotions. We all have difficult feelings, but we also know sometimes it's difficult not to give in to despair.

My father's journal cries out desperately for creative expression. He writes that he never explored his creative potential. He saw this final stage of his life as an opportunity to explore what he calls "unborn" talent.

We all possess creative talent, and in many of us, there is a strong urge to be creative, to express ourselves in meaningful ways. I see these deep longings in everyone. No matter who we are or how old we are, we long to express ourselves.

But where to begin?

Well, maybe I should know. After all, I have been a creative person all my life. I chose a creative career and consider myself a creative professional which means that I utilize a creative process in my work. But all of us, those who write music, design objects, shape sculptures, click photographs, write novels, or put form to canvas, will tell you the same thing about creativity: it's about emotional risk, more specifically facing your fears.

I will tell you the honest truth: every time I face the blank page, I turn myself inside out. Creative people become expert at accessing their vulnerabilities; it's what allows the creation of serious, long-lasting art; it's what allows the real truth to be uncovered; it's what makes being creative addictive, exhilarating, and painful.

Emotional risk is what I do as an artist. I pick away at memory. I focus intensely on what I don't understand. At my best and most courageous, I plunge into my own fears.

Of course, not all creative people are into this type of torture, but many understand that in order to find truth and beauty, you have to work at it. I know many budding artists who want to produce that hit record, beautiful painting, or unforgettable screenplay without understanding that the creative process requires one to be true to the landscape of soul, not the shrill of the marketplace.

Creative people, especially those who haven't yet found their medium or a confidence in exploring their own sense of expression, often find it difficult to begin. After all, what is a more awesome task than facing the proverbial blank canvas?

If you want to put pressure on someone, tell him or her this: "You're fortunate; you have the freedom to do or achieve whatever you want." Instead of this, you might ask questions like this: What kinds of experiences have you had that filled you with the most joy? What have you done in your life that occupied you to the maximum and made time melt away?

Be careful not to discount anybody's answers to these questions. Being creative is absolutely not the province of what our society deems as artistically valuable. Any task can be accomplished with creativity. An artist isn't someone who necessarily sells the work; an artist can be someone who pursues enlightenment through any task or activity. I have met artists who were engineers, teachers, gardeners, lawyers, parents, welders, and salespeople.

When it comes to expressing yourself as an artist, it's not what you do, but how you do it. Creative people often utilize a process that helps them explore ideas, choices, and questions. My own process is really quite simple: first I write down as freely as possible every single possibility I can collect. I take this brainstorming phase more seriously than most. I have notebooks filled with brainstorming, clustering, note taking, and doodling.

The second phase is questioning. Without choosing a possibility, I begin asking questions. Here is where you really have to listen to your feelings and not just your analytical side. I ask questions that have to do with assessing the depth of an idea or choice. I ask myself what scares me the most. Also, I look for things that others might throw away. For example, I consciously seek misunderstanding, confusion and doubt. These areas are like gold mines. What you think you understand is often the last place to find your treasure. Instead, go exactly where a person like you would never look.

The act of creation seems like the first stage to many, but it is really the last stage. My family knows that an artist works at the oddest times and in the oddest ways. I take notes in the movie theatre. I speak into my tape recorder in the middle of the night. My wife will tell you that I, the grumpiest soul in the world, takes looking out the window very seriously.

Unfortunately, I never had a discussion with my father about these things. I read his journal now, and I feel how afraid he was about exploring his own soul. I wonder how many people out there want and need to explore their artistic potential. If you do, I encourage you to share your desire with someone you care about. Beyond fear, there is great freedom, accomplishment, and joy.

Friendship

Anyone ever pick your nose? Well, if you're wrapped in a body cast with a broken neck and four screws in your lobes, a little dig might be quite a relief; it's definitely a favour you might ask a really close friend.

Anyone ever bust you out of prison? Do you know someone who has the skills to lead the team of mercenaries dedicated to your prison break? "Lock and load," says my cousin Henry. He would gladly pull a grenade pin with his teeth, but only for the F-Team, his family.

Do you know a doctor? You need to know a doctor. What if you're hit with flesh-eating disease? You need a pal to make sure they cut off the correct limb. My friend Dr. Dave has helped my family survive paper cuts, terminal illness, and weird little bumps under the scrotum.

Speaking of the lower anatomy, you also need to befriend a lawyer. We live in an age of litigation. People will threaten to sue your ass for anything. The other day, my left ass wanted to sue my right ass. This is why you need a lawyer like my neighbour: a man with a sphincter made of Rhino Liner.

Ever look at an invoice and choke? Having a mechanic or a journeyman around is very useful. This is especially true for people with graduate degrees, whose limited practical skills include typing, arguing about nothing and, under close supervision, loading the dishwasher.

My wife thinks I solve all dilemmas by writing cheques, Googling, or emailing friends for advice. I am spectacularly unhandy. My idea of plumbing is flushing twice. I am told, however, that I'm quite excellent at standing by the chip dip at parties. Do not attempt this; it's only for academics with years of specialized training.

"Food taster. That's all we need you for," says Dr. Dave. "Face it. You're useless," states my cousin Henry. "Stand back and watch me," says my wife. "The forks go in upside down."

Friendship is like a lottery. Basically, you luck out. People sail randomly in and out of your life. Unless you have a strategy, you don't choose your friends. Fate does. We befriend people because we bump into them. Someone moves in next door; soon you're swapping kids and hot tub fluids. Do you have a friendship strategy?

Some say friendship is an art and not a matter of chance, geography and convenience.

I'm told that the art of having a friend is the art of being a friend. I don't think being a friend is that simple, especially being a true friend.

I know this because I am a crummy friend. I have jerk genes. I don't send Christmas cards. I love silence. I hate answering the phone. I freeze like a deer in the headlights when a stranger smiles. I run from my feelings. I let friendships wither because I am so stinking gutless.

Worse, I often make friendships for bad reasons. I think about what a particular person might be able to offer me. These friendships begin with insincerity, especially on my part. They are "dealships," temporary alliances, based upon supporting some mutually beneficial agenda. You scratch my scrotum – I'll scratch ... the wrinkly spot of your choice.

Many relationships are based on this economic formula of mutual self-interest. Will these deal-ships last? Usually we are "pals" until one of us doesn't need the other. Others are very good about growing these deal-ships into something real and genuine.

My resolution this year is to be a better friend. "Don't bother," says Dave. "Focus on your family." My cousin says not to bother, "Listen, dude, you're not that likeable, so get over yourself." My best friend, the woman who married me, suggests that friendship isn't just making new friends; it's deciding which friendships to keep.

When I was a kid, we moved a lot. I went to nine schools. My father was a wanderer, a United Church minister with itchy feet. For Christmas, I only wanted – and always got – Lego. On birthdays, I had but one wish. Every birthday of my childhood, nearly every November of my life, I hoped, I prayed, I wanted only one thing: a friend.

Today I still enjoy some of the very friendships that started in elementary school. As a father of two young children, I find myself wishing the same thing for them. "You are my best friend" – when is the last time you heard more powerful words?

When my son sees his best friend, his eyes glow like radioactive matter. Remember what it was like to have someone to share every inane thought? Who do you like? Who do you hate? Who do you sort of really *kind of* like? Can Batman beat up Spiderman without Robin?

When we grow older, friendships seem to mean less, especially if we are busy building families and business relationships. Life gets crowded; just being true to those we are related to, or in business with, takes it toll. Who has the time to initiate, build, and maintain friendships?

Your friends tell you who you are. If they are true friends, they can sing your praises *and* spill the painful truth. And more importantly, your true friend will still be your friend after you share your sorrows, joys, and mistakes.

What is true friendship? A friend isn't just someone who can do you a favour, like your mechanic, mercenary, or immediate supervisor. A true friend is someone who will accept you as you are, even after putting up bail. Sorry, all you economists, friendship is more than a self-interested exchange.

Some people go through friends like toilet paper. If we remain quick to be offended, what does that say about our chances for a civil society? We are not just talking about friendship here; we're talking about politics, world peace, and fewer heart attacks.

By the way, when is the last time you made a new friend or called an old one? When is the last time, you took a friendship to the next level? Maybe I'm vain, but I'd like a big funeral – for my friends.

May you, me, and the world find true friendship.

Do Not Fly Away

*"In Canada, suicide is the leading cause of death for men aged 25
to 29 and 40 to 44, and for women aged 30 to 34. It is the second
leading cause of death among youth aged 15 to 24. For each
completed suicide there are 100 attempts, and over 23,000
Canadians are hospitalized each year for a suicide attempt."*
— SAFETY-COUNCIL.ORG

His body was found hanging in a basement utility closet. I talked
with him the night before. His voice sounded bright and sincere, as
it usually did. He told me everything would be okay, that he was set,
that plans had been made. Hey man, he had said.

What's up?

Everything is fine here, he said. Just wanted to say ... just
wanted to ... Then his voice cracked. Thank you.

For what? I said.

For, you know, being a good teacher to me.

My eyes filled up then, as they always do when I think of these
words, and I wanted to hold him tight. Hold him tight so he would
not fly away.

But we were on the telephone. So I did this: not much of anything.

Well, I said with forced cheer. I'll talk to you later. I needed to
escape his gratitude. (I still keep the letter he wrote me in a desk
drawer, and I have only read it once.) He was too much for me, this
big kid.

Why was I always so afraid that he was going to say something
sincere to me?

Just a second, he said. There was a pause in the line. I thought I could hear him answering the door. Pizza delivery? I could hear traffic in the distance. His apartment was near Broadway. Maybe it was raining, too? Was that the sound of an electric trolley bus, the wires sparking and twitching overhead?

A few months before he called, we met in Prince George for the last time. It was spring but still felt like winter. The last bit of grey snow remained in the ditches. He took the bus up to see his mother. She was having a tough time. He'd lost his younger brother the year before in a car accident. His mother was now living alone in a single-wide trailer in College Heights. He told me about sitting with her. She talked endlessly about his younger brother while wiping tears with one hand and holding a cigarette and a glass of sherry in another. She's creating mythology, he said.

Is she going to hold up? I asked while we walked the grounds of the college where I worked.

She feels stunned and blown away, he said. Dad is right out of it, too, but he's busy paying for what's-her-face's manicures and day care.

Wow, I said. Can things unravel any more?

It's like my brother was all that was holding us together, he said. My older brother won't talk to me. My mother is a mess. And Dad has a new family now. He's dying his hair. He's driving a truck. We're like oil and water now. Dispersing.

I'm sorry, I said.

It was a blue sky day. A distant blue like you only see in the North. The cars and logging trucks roared along the bypass that cut through the middle of town. He wore corduroys and brown suede shoes with crepe soles. I grabbed his arm and steered him away from some dog droppings.

May in Prince George is fragrant, he said. Pulp mill combined with thawing dog crap.

Yeah, I said. It's spring.

You don't have to worry about me.

I've known you since you were nineteen, I said. What are you, twenty-six now?

I have to tell you something, he said and stopped. I listened to him tell me about a series of appointment, he had had with a psychiatrist.

How does the medication make you feel?

I don't know. Like tasting through gauze. Like being underwater. All the usual pharmacological clichés.

Can you stand it?

I don't know.

What does the doctor say?

He says I might be medicated for the rest of my life. Let me put it this way: It's not getting any better. I have a psychological illness. I can't hold a thought.

That's terrible.

I looked at him. He was tall and handsome, his smile broad and genuine. People loved him. He could talk with anybody.

I should get going, I said. I knew that I should have said something more, done something different than what I actually did which was just to stand there and look up the Nechako river cut banks and the spirals of white smoke coming up from the pulp mill.

You know much about pain? he asked suddenly.

What I know about pain isn't very insightful.

Sometimes I hear voices, he said.

What do they say?

They say that when you're in pain you wonder if you can stand another minute.

* * *

I can barely remember his roommate who told me that they had found his body. She was new, somebody who didn't know him well. She called and told me, and I didn't know what to do with the information.

He talked about you, she said.

I'm just a teacher of his, I said. I talked with him the night before.

He said nice things about you, she said.

* * *

There was no funeral to attend. No memorial service. At the time, I didn't know how common this was. We just don't know how to handle suicide. We are at once sad, guilty, and ashamed.

I wanted to call his friends and let them know, but since I was only a teacher, I didn't really know his current circle. I wanted to do a lot of things. In short, I did nothing.

When I think about this boy, this tall, beautiful boy, I think about his journey. He was the first in his family to go to university, the first in his family to prefer deconstructing poetry to slapping a puck. He put his sensitivities to use at university. He showed me A+ essays he had received in both sociology and English; he talked about a future as a lawyer. He talked about making his mother proud.

I thought I sat on the outskirts of his life, but I realize now that I was wrong. I was his teacher and teachers can play a central role, even if the contact is infrequent. But this is not a story about teachers.

There is a story to every suicide. For many, his loss is a riddle to be solved, even if for me the answer to the riddle is quite mundane. But his life is not a detective story. This is not a story about why.

In the letter that he wrote me, the letter that I have had the courage to read only once, he tells me that "we all have a reckless disregard for love." His mother loved him, but could only talk about his lost brother. His older brother loved him, but could not understand his pain. His father loved him, but only at a safe distance.

There is no one to blame. We have all lost people. We still feel their absence. I miss him, even though he has been gone for many years. I don't care so much about the details of what happened because I care more about who he was. I care about what he could have been. I care about what he meant to me.

In the corridors and corners of my heart, he walks with me just as he did that spring afternoon in Prince George. I hear his footsteps beside mine. I hear him laugh and smile.

I am gone away, he says. But you are a part of me.

I whisper his name in the mornings between sleep and walking. I love you. You honoured me by calling me teacher. And I don't blame myself anymore for you being gone.

STAN CHUNG

This Moment for the Rest of My Life

It wasn't supposed to be particularly memorable. It wasn't sunny. It wasn't cloudy. It wasn't exciting. It wasn't boring. It just wasn't much of anything.

So ... I decided to do something that I had never done before and have never done since. I decided this while sitting on the steps of our home at 299 Third Avenue North in Williams Lake.

I questioned myself; this moment was as good as any other. What was so wrong with this moment? Nothing. Absolutely nothing.

I sat on the worn concrete steps of our house. I glanced at my running shoes, faded jeans, striped shirt, and scrawny arms. The wind pushed back the black bangs that covered my forehead. I wore a blue Adidas jacket with three yellow stripes along the sleeves. The stripes were more mustard than yellow because nobody knew how to wash these jackets without running the yellow into the blue.

In front of me rested my trusty steed, the olive green mustang mount with the white vinyl banana seat, chrome sissy bar, and red STP stickers. It was a good bike. We ordered it from Sears, and it had served me without complaint for almost three years.

So, I said to myself, with as much resolve as an eleven-year-old boy can muster, I'm going to memorize this moment for the rest of my life.

This moment. This moment. This moment. For the rest of my life.

There is no other moment, I realized. I have no other life. This is it. Right here. Right now. In this very spot in the universe, feeling exactly the way I feel right now, which to be precise is not exactly much of anything. But I pushed forward and tried to understand my particular time and place in the universe.

Latitude: 52.1333413

Longitude: -122.1444031

Elevation: 609 m

Time: Oct. 11, 1973, around 11:42 a.m..

In 1973, at the above mentioned space and time, I was in Mrs. Buchanan's grade five class. My best friend was Andy Gibbs. I lived with my parents in a house called the manse right beside St. Andrew's United Church. My father was a minister. My mother was studying bookkeeping twice a week. We ate Swanson's Hungry Man dinners on Tuesday nights and cardboard pizzas on Thursdays. I was having trouble with long division. I really liked this girl. Her name was Sherrin Takahashi. I wondered if my cat, Dusty, would ever come back. This stuff I just wrote. I didn't really think. Those are just the facts that surround the thinking.

Okay, this is what I thought.

I'm not very powerful. I'm just a kid. But I'm not filled with how great I am or how pathetic I am. I'm not dissatisfied or filled with emptiness. I'm not thinking about what I will become or how I will become what I become. I'm not trying to feel the sensuality of the wind, sultry movement of the planet, or inhale the fragrance of grass, honeysuckle, or dandelion green. October smells. No, I'm not thinking or feeling these things. I'm not thinking. I'm not feeling. I'm not. I'm not. I'm not. I'm in a state of "notiness." Ha!

I was existing, capital b, Being. The eleven-year-old boy was making time sit still as a reference point of consciousness, a GPS marker of his life, for what, I don't know. (So many things that the boy doesn't know, will never know, doesn't ever want to know.) There are so many things that I, the grown man, don't know. This moment of impermanence, this fixing of eternity, this conscious experiment with memory was, for me, my first and best recognition that there is no point in wishing or dreaming about another life, no point in wasting moments wanting things to be other than they are, that the greatest sin in life was feeling insufficient, that living wasn't sufficient, more than enough.

Now I am a man, a middle-aged man with a paunch and a bundle of insufficiencies. The eleven-year-old boy reminds me that I am not my victories, economic gains, public profile, or reputation. I am not any of these things. When the strengths are gone, when the legs are weak, when the mind goes soft, then what am I? Can I be more than the words on my business card? What, then, is identity? And, if the question is even worthy of pursuit, does identity matter?

Now I am my father. An old man. I smell like I don't want to smell. The air is cold to me now. All is air. Everything is seen through my cold eye. I am strong. Nothing moves me. I am cool. I am too calm. My legs are swinging to and fro. I am in a coffee shop reading a book of poems. What does each poem say? It says, "Shut the F up." It says, You can't do it. It says, You don't know enough. I am an old man now, I guess, so careful with my farts. Every person is a missed possibility, every thought a winding path of distraction.

Life alone is not good enough, he says. I'm isolated from that guy, myself. Every day I'm in a coffee shop, wanting to cry. I miss the way I never was. A woman with a stroller comes in, the big baby sitting up right, taking in the world, drinking from the fire hose of life, so the cliché goes. Sit down and breathe, big little one. Take it all in. Oh, my mother, long ago dead, I hear your joy in the chatter of friends meeting for a cup of tea. Show them your love, my mother tells me from the warm salt ocean of death. Tears in my eyes again. How to love? That's the only question. Why do I always remember, when it is too late, all the things I should have done?

Remember that eleven-year-old boy who wanted to live deeply, to live sunk in the moment, sunk so deep? The boy is afraid of dying. Really. The boy doesn't know he is sorry for himself. The boy is mourning the man he will be. That boy was the best of me. The very best of me.

It wasn't sunny. It wasn't cloudy. It wasn't exciting. It wasn't boring. It was now, everything, all of life itself. The boy calls to me when I bother to listen: this life. This life! This life!

3 x 1973: Williams Lake – Part I

I fell in love three times when I was in grade six. The first time was Sherrin T. She wore round, wire-framed glasses that slid down her cute nose. She laughed a lot and once got hiccups on the phone. Oh, they sounded so cute. Like a mouse burping.

After school I used to sneak over to the basement of our church and phone her while my sister practiced the piano upstairs.

"What are you doing, Sherrin?"

"Thinking."

"About what?" "I don't know if I should tell you." I could hear her breathing. She was living in a mobile home up near the hospital. I imagined she sat on shag carpet that her mom made her rake every day.

"Tell me, please, Sherrin."

"I was thinking about how much I like you." I sat down on the floor and closed my eyes when I heard this. Upstairs I could hear my sister pack up her books and close the piano lid.

"I like you, too," I finally said.

"Do you like me or do you LIKE-LIKE me?" I breathed for a little while and twisted the long black cord.

"I like-like you."

"Yeah," she said. "I really like-like you."

"Yeah," I said feeling all stuck inside.

"Just yeah or YEAH-YEAH?" she said.

A few phone calls later, she told me the terrible news. "We're moving north of town. And Mom says I've got to change schools. My last name won't be the same either."

"Wait!" I said. "What? You're moving? What do you mean to-day was your last day?" When you're a grade-sixer at Marie Sharpe Elementary School in Williams Lake BC, you live for two things. One is knocking someone off the sloped logs while playing king of the mountain on the new adventure playground, or being chased by at least three girls into the Big Tire. The Big Tire was dark, filled with wood chips, and smelled a bit like cat pee, and, well, the true essence of genuine rubber. The Big Tire was our board room, our executive suite. This is where we talked at recess and lunch. Who wanted a cigarette? Who wanted to play spin the bottle in the bush? Where do you get those North Star Runners? And just who was goin' around with who?

The Big Tire also had a very cool echo. It made you sound like you were on radio. Ladies and Gentlemen, I love Sherrin T!

I thought I had found perfection. After all, she was half-Japa-nese. I liked that about her. We looked like two of a kind. My oval Korean-face with the straight black bangs and charcoal eyes and her brown hair, round cheeks, and soft eyes.

When I finally said goodbye to Sherrin while sitting in the dark church basement, not listening to my sister's constant pentatonic scales, I chickened out. I so wanted to tell her how I felt. How I had this vague sense of our future.

It's way more than like-like, I wanted to say. It's ...

Later that night, I climbed out of my bedroom window onto the sturdy crook of the elm tree. The leaves whispered and shimmered above me. It was dark and cool and smelled like damp grass. The crickets were calling and the universe was aching.

You are eleven years old. You wanted to say things, but you couldn't. You'll never see her again. You'll forget her face. The way she blinked and giggled. How her eyelashes curled. This is why you're crying. She was just like you. Japanese is close enough. You could maybe find her again some day. I cried like a baby for three nights and then, bang, click, spin, I moved on. Her name was Cindy Z. Oh, Cindy. Cindy Z. She wore jean jackets. She smoked. Lived in an apartment near Boitano Park, and she scared everyone. Her eyes were emeralds. Yes, she wore an actual bra and needed it. And rumour was that she'd had her period. Whatever that was.

Cindy Z sat in front of me. Her reddish-brown hair flowed down her back. It wasn't long before I was continuously dropping my Pink Pearl eraser so she'd pick it up.

"Thanks," I said.

"For the sixteenth time, you're welcome."

Five minutes later, I'd do it again. Mrs. Buchanan was busy trying to teach us long division. I will never learn long division, I thought. Who cares? I'm too busy sniffing Cindy Z. She smelled like cigarettes, suede, and cinnamon Dentyne. It made me feel all squirmy.

Cindy and I lasted. I asked her to the big fall sock hop. That was no easy task. I even phoned her John Wayne-style from our kitchen in the manse.

"Hey, Cindy."

"Yeah."

"You wanna go to the dance with me?"

"Yeah."

"Okay, bye." Click.

Cindy and I danced. We really danced. I remember putting my thumbs in her belt loops and pulling her close to me. We were in our white sock feet. We were eleven years old. Okay, she maybe was a bit older. "Don't talk," she said. Her mouth was hot on my ear.

We made the earth move and we could feel the rhythm of the universe. I held her hips until I could smell the green apple shampoo in her hair. The music played. A single phonograph with a 45 record wobbling around and around. A suitcase speaker blaring the hit by Edward Bear.

It's the last song. It's the last song I'll ever write for you.

Cindy scared me and she knew it. Once Mrs. Buchanan moved our desks apart, we were like Romeo and Juliet. Fate had intervened! How would we survive! Could I toss my eraser or ruler across two rows for a visit?

I hatched a plan. Cindy sat near the pencil sharpener. Between November and February, I ground down a forest of pencils to be near her. I cranked. I spun lead. I rotated HB.

"Why you need more pencils?" Mom asked. "What you do with so many?"

"Fate, Mommy," I said. "Fate."

In February, something weird happened. Cindy Z and I had played out our hand. We were getting ready to see other people, explore our options, play the field. Kid stuff.

"We're moving," I finally told Cindy. "Up on Pigeon Avenue. I'll be attending Cataline for grade seven."

"That's crappy," she said. "I don't know if I'm going to school next year. Mom wants me to help her out at home."

Cindy's mom was sick or something. She kept the drapes drawn.

"Mom's got the blues again," she'd say.

So? Well, there was Janet, the beautiful girl from the sweet and sour restaurant. There was the long-legged Theresa O. Long blond hair. She lived right across the parking lot from the War Memorial Rink. Practically neighbours.

But in February of 1973, something else happened. I fell for a third time. At first, she was the biggest nuisance ever. This little, black-haired plain girl. This quiet little girl from the restaurant on Third known as Sam's. She smelled of deep-fried pork, Breck shampoo, and red licorice. She never said a word to me all year, but she would change my life. Then and now and forever. And I'm talking forever-forever. Her name was ...

STAN CHUNG

3 x 1973: Williams Lake – Part II

Lilac, the intoxicating sweet fragrance of lilac, makes you think of the three girls you loved in 1973.

Oh, you will always respond to the smell of lilac. The curve of a young girl's lips. The softness of a summer breeze.

A whirlwind spins dust in the parking lot of War Memorial Rink. It touches down. Lifts off. It moves toward a clothesline carousel in the neighbour's yard.

You sit on your bike with one foot on a pedal and another on the curb. In the distance, she is walking away from you.

Her name is Jean Yee and you have broken her heart.

She is walking down Third Avenue, a long road that bisects the town. It begins in the south where apartment buildings sit between one-story houses. The road then stretches north through the only stoplight in town and moves upward to new subdivisions.

You live on this road, in a little manse beside the church. Later, you will live hours farther up Highway 97 to the spruce capital of Prince George. On December 27, 1988, you will be getting off the bus in minus 40 holding suitcases and your first generation computer. You will be 26.

The small whirlwind spins up bits of dust and corrals newspaper. The swirl spins the clothesline carousel with its circular patchwork of sheets and towels.

Then it is suddenly gone. You notice a white butterfly hovering above the clover.

Time past. Time present. Time future. You know time is not a straight road like Third Avenue. Time is more like a clothesline turning in the breeze and becoming a butterfly.

You need her now. You need her now.

But now is decades away. The young girl walking away sits across the row from you in Mrs. Singlehurst's class. She says hello to you each morning. She lets you borrow her wooden ruler with the metal edge that she keeps in a hand sewn-pencil case.

She flips her long black hair. And again. You could count to ten as the shiny black hair falls back into place.

For Christmas, she gives you a white peace symbol on a chain to hang around your neck. No girl has ever given you a thing before. On Valentine's Day she comes by the house. There are tiny icicles hanging above the door.

Your mother calls you by your Korean name. "Sae-Hoon-ah!"

"What?"

"Jean is here."

"Jean who?"

"Come here." She grabs you by the neck. Jean passes you a gift wrapped in pink. It is the size of a cereal box. Did she buy you Captain Crunch?

"Thanks."

"And here," Jean says. You take three red carnations. You hand them to your shocked mother.

The flowers do not register for decades. Jean steps away from the door. Your mother says goodbye and says goodbye again. Your mother watches her from the living room window.

"Wave at her! Silly boy. Sae-Hoon-ah!"

"What's in the box?"

You tear it open. Inside the box is a miniature chest of drawers made of dark wood. There are twelve little drawers. In each drawer, there is an urn, a pot, or something else made of gleaming brass.

"What is it?"

"It is so nice," she says. "It is so nice."

Your mother keeps Jean Yee's valentine present until well after you graduate from high school. It is still in the house after you graduate from university. After graduate school in Toronto it is still in the house — under your mother's bed where she hides the gold jewelry.

Your mother has passed on into the river of love, but you think she probably still has this miniature set of drawers somewhere.

"It is so nice," you can hear her say.

You, on the other hand, could not care less. Not for the gift. Not for Jean. Not for her love.

What is wrong with you?

You watch her walking down the street on this June day in 1973. You don't know that you will never see her again. You don't even know that you don't know what love is.

Jean Yee watches you at the dance with Cindy Z. She sees you running to the Big Tire with Sherrin T.

She goes straight home after school to sit with her sister in the restaurant doing her homework, wiping tables, pouring coffee and doing what daughters do in restaurants owned by their parents.

You do not know about those who love you first. If someone loves you first in 1973 during Watergate and Kung Fu fighting and Crocodile Rock, well, you just might be loved – forever.

You do not know this as she walks away. You do not know this for years and years until you are a man.

When you are a grown man and you travel on Highway 97, you always go past Sam's Restaurant. Most of the time you drive by slowly, imagining that somehow she is still in there, sitting at the counter, watching the twelve-inch black and white, serving chicken chow mein to ranchers out east or the loggers in Horsefly or miners out at Gibraltar or families off the reserve.

And one time, years later, when you are a man, you pull up to the restaurant and ask to see the owner.

"How's it going?"

"Long as the weather holds up for Stampede."

"Remember a Chinese family that used to own this place?"

"Yes, sir. Mister Yee. Bit before my time."

"You remember the girls? The two sisters? Ever remember what happened to them?"

"Nope. Sorry, can't says I do."

"All right. Maybe a coffee and some fries with gravy then?"

"You remember the girl, do you?"

"Yeah, I do. The younger one. I can't hardly forget."

"Been there, brother. Been there."

You never found Jean Yee. And what would you say if you did? Maybe you would say thank you and sorry at the same time.

Thank you for your love. And sorry I did not love you back.

But I understand a lot more now, you would say. About time. About memories. About the true nature of love.

And what would she say to you? Would she remember you, that skinny Korean boy with black bangs who did not listen to his mother?

"You see? She looks like us. Maybe she wants to fit into this strange stampede town. Like you. Maybe she's just like you?"

Truthfully, she loved you differently.

It was a kind of love that you didn't know how to accept. And still don't.

Love can be like a gift you do not think you deserve, especially love that is offered without condition. This is exactly the kind of love you once felt in Korea before your mother left you at the age of three to settle in Canada.

Your mother loved you and left you. And even though you learned a year later that she did not abandon you, how would you ever learn to accept love again?

In 1973 your heart opens. But not wide enough. It is she who teaches you, then and now and forever, that your heart needs to learn one simple and impossible thing.

You are worthy of love.

Oh, Jean Yee. Oh, beautiful, gentle and quiet Jean Yee. Is it too late to tell you why I could not receive your love?

There she is. She is walking down Third Avenue away from you.

Looking into the Mirror

On Monday, Cho Seung-Hui killed 32 people at Virginia Tech, in what is being called the largest mass murder in American history.

The tragedy at Virginia Tech can teach us a lot about ourselves, even though we may want to avert our gaze. On the surface, it appears we are nothing like Mr. Cho: we think he is probably an aberration, a freak, a psycho, a mad man. You see them at the movies all the time. They are not like you and me.

Others say, look at Dawson College in Montreal. Look at Columbine. Look at Tabor. What is going on with our young men? Could it happen here?

Look, look, look. What did these killers see? How do we see them? Our visual culture, the dominance of our vision in apprehending reality, may form part of the answer to our questions.

Take a look at the picture beside my name. What do you see? I am male, Korean-born, and wear glasses. Do I possess the face of a killer? How would I look with my arms raised, pistols in my hands, as Mr. Cho appeared on many media front pages?

Might you think me the hero of some action movie? Might you see me as a victim of a masculine gun culture, perpetrated by a blood-soaked media? Might you look twice at guys that look like me? Would you feel your back shiver at the next slightly studious, Asian male you see on the sidewalk?

I doubt you see me as a sex symbol. You will not see me as the next American Idol, the next Stanley Cup MVP, or the next stud doctor on House or ER. Asian males, especially those in commercial movies, are the sidekick, the bad guy, or the best friend. We only get the hot voluptuous woman with the mighty hair and chest, if, and only if, we hold a gun to her head.

Another way of doing it, of course, is to make a ton of money, so much loot that cleavage, horsepower, and status are only a line of credit away. But, to rephrase the words of Lennon and McCartney, can money buy me love?

You are going to hear much talk about race and class when it comes to Mr. Cho. But you're not going to hear a lot about overt racism. When I grew up in the seventies in Williams Lake, I was called every name in the book. Nobody calls me names anymore, but that doesn't mean there aren't still subtle forms of excluding people on the basis of race or class.

"We don't want to hire her; she won't fit in." "It's his thick accent. He's different." "I don't like her skirt; she won't fit into our culture." Have you heard statements like this?

While we live in as tolerant a society as any, this doesn't mean we always do a good job making people feel welcome. Sometimes ignoring someone, not seeing them, is as hurtful as calling them a racist epithet. It is especially easy, when they reject us to say, "Them foreigners aren't as friendly as they could be. Where's their gratitude? We let 'em into the country, didn't we?"

When I look into the mirror, what do I see? I do not see a slender Asian guy with bad eyes, a flat ass, and skinny wrists. When I look at published pictures of Mr. Cho with his greasy forehead and round, wire-framed glasses, I see a boy who wants to be a man.

But what kind of man?

In our culture, violence and masculinity are nearly inseparable. Our dads expected us boys not to cry, to be tough, to shake it off. We learn by six how to drop the gloves; after all, we see it every Saturday on Hockey Night in Canada. Boys who can't take a hit, shake off a bloody nose, or stand up for their sisters are labeled sissy or worse.

You want to be a man? You have to be ready to fight. Whether you're six or sixty, boys and men are expected to be ready to use their fists. It's women and girls to the life rafts; the men and boys go down with the ship.

What if you're not physically strong? What if you're really scared? You can take the name-calling, the homophobia, the lack of social self-assurance and join a gym, or you can take the easy route — buy yourself a weapon.

When I was kid, everyone expected me to be a natural martial arts champion because of the "slant of my eyes." So, I took karate. I did push ups. I pumped iron. I went to kung fu movies, worshipped Bruce Lee, and practiced killing people in my dreams. Bruce Lee, oh, Bruce, you gave balls to all the skinny-assed pansies in the world.

But as I got older, I wondered if a Canadian girl would ever go to the prom with me. My family didn't have much money either. My clothing lacked brand name appeal. I walked to school; the macho rich guys drove Z28s.

At university, I realized that I needed three extra jobs to keep up. Cars, gas, dinners out — it all cost plenty. So do moonlight drinks quaffed at bush parties and hotel bars. University costs a lot more than tuition and books.

In the late eighties, I dated a woman who flatly told me after I'd met her parents that her parents didn't think I had much long-term wedding potential. "'Teacher' isn't exactly a high-paying profession," she told me.

After I introduced her to my parents, she looked at me and said that she was glad they didn't look like the people who ran the corner grocery store; apparently, my folks didn't reek of garlic. I went home, looked into the bathroom mirror, and wondered what was wrong with me.

Time passes and you grow up. You discover that there is strength in kindness, and you find someone to share your life with. Every morning I see in the bathroom mirror a very happy man who works hard, loves his wife and children, and lives in the most multicultural country on earth. But others don't see me that way. At a writer's conference in Banff, a very famous writer singled me out and asked to speak to me privately.

"What can I do for you," I said. "Do you know me?"

"You look like you can fix computers. Would you help me with my printer?"

The total picture of Mr. Cho is one filled with contradictions. He wanted love and acceptance from a culture that celebrates violence and cheerfulness. He was identified as someone who needed help, but did he receive it?

It seems from the early accounts that Mr. Cho was tossed back and forth like someone whom nobody cares about, like someone whose problems are not our problems. He was on a merry-go-round of referrals. They knew he was troubled; the early signs were evident.

We can look at gender, race, and cultural issues until the cows come home, but you'd be right if you pointed out that this might be a straight case of mental illness. You can say, if you want, that the health care system failed Mr. Cho.

But what exactly is a health care system?

My wife believes a health care system is a loving family and a truly supportive community where there is a seamless integration of professionals from social workers, to the justice sphere, to the hospitals and clinics.

Maybe the problem is not that Mr. Cho was Korean, or a loner, or a male. The real problem was the social stigma surrounding mental illness and the lack of therapeutic resources in a pay-as-you-go health care system.

There was no one to watch his back. No one to slap him on the back and hold a mirror up to his behaviour. No advocate to guide him through the complex network of health professionals. No one to hold him tight and whisper, "I will be there for you. We will get you the right kind of help. I'll see you through."

Don't misunderstand me. This is not an exercise in advocating for a murderer or pointing the finger at those who sincerely tried to help; I despise what Mr. Cho did. On the contrary, this column is not so much about Mr. Cho as it's about me.

What would I do if I met someone like Mr. Cho? How would I help him? How would I make sure I did not fail him? And, finally, a question for you: what would you do if he were me or someone who looked just like me?

GLOBAL CITIZEN

The Forbidden
Cheezie

Take Oprah. Rich and powerful. This woman can have everything she wants. She employs a chef to stock her pantry and cook for her. Another employee takes her to the gym. Her loyal staff pamper her every whim. Every day on television, Oprah, the mighty Oprah, the post-laundry president of the TV world, preaches transformation to millions of viewers who want to be Oprah-sized rich and Oprah-sized beautiful and Oprah-sized happy. But nobody is more dissatisfied with being Oprah-sized than Oprah herself.

It seems that Oprah, oh so rich, oh so powerful, is no more powerful than the nearest Cheezie. Oprah is a bit of tub, you see, and there seems to be nothing she can do about it.

I don't know about you, but if Oprah can't lose a few pounds, the world is in deep trouble. Here is a woman, a very powerful woman, a woman admired and successful, but she cannot really change herself in the most fundamental of ways. No matter what, she cannot resist the urge to be what she is: smart, beautiful, and a little chunky.

The cynic in me asks if Oprah can't change, why should you or I? If Oprah can't change herself, how can she change the world? After all, the great Ghandi exhorts us "to be the change we want to see in the world."

As much as I admire Oprah, her good works, her focus on good books, her support of the idealist Obama, I wonder, especially after her crazy new night-time show where charitable behaviour has a million dollar impact, if Oprah is really helping us poor slobs. Is watching television and buying her magazine a good way to become

151

a global citizen, a champion of yourself and the unwashed? Is going Oprah anything more than a savvy addictive formula for telling you to be dissatisfied with yourself, with the colour of your hair, the breadth of your library, the size of thighs?

If you are in the forest and nobody hears the sound of your thighs rubbing together, does that mean your chubbiness does not really exist? Of course, deep in the forest, you're not going find any plasma flat screens. There is only one channel when you get outside: the here and now. Things happen slowly and the colours aren't as sharp as HD. It can be terrifying.

Yes, I admit it. I have measured out my life in episodes of Law and Order. I grew up on television, and I admit that I'm a helpless addict. I have the audio visual equipment and the sedentary evenings to prove it. Like any addict, all I can do is manage it; get my fix as quickly and efficiently as possible. I skip commercials. I try not to watch forensic porn or anything involving voting someone off. And yes, I do watch Oprah once in awhile. It's research, I tell you! I'm a cultural academic, an impassionate observer of the human condition. I really like Doc Oz!

So let's give the woman a break. Oprah is splendidly human, so change is just as difficult for her as it for us. Just like you or I, she puts on her support hose one leg at a time. I confess right now. I couldn't lose twenty pounds, if my life depended it. I haven't given up on exercising for I know it is a mandatory part of life. I just can't give up on Oreos or those designer jelly beans or chocolate pudding. I just can't give up on crispy chow mein. I just can't give up on the soul-gratifying substance known as bacon, or as they like to call it, the US, Canadian bacon.

Even just typing the word "bacon" puts my brain in a sensual state of uncontrollable longing. Bacon, bacon, bacon. Try it with scallops. Or salad or ice cream. Try it naked.

Food habits die hard. I know people who salt their food with maniacal hyper-precision. My old friend, Ron, dips individual fries into ketchup and then into a pile of salt. Another pal of mine, a guy with no tastebuds, must end each day with a litre of Coke and a towering seven-inch pile of pure Pringles. Me, I'm no better. Ask my wife: I have few hobbies outside of playing tennis, watching Idol (for cultural scholarship), and searching for that perfect shrimp tempura.

My darn belly has been growing and it can't be stopped. I pat the darn thing and ask it to stop growing, but it just won't listen. My digestion problems have been increasing, too. I'm backed up, I'm not backed up, I'm backed up again — oh, geez, it must be Wednesday — time to have a long sit down. I rotate on a lunar cycle. While I try to eat organic and local, I often sneak out of my office and head for the nearest all-you-can-eat fish and chips. What can I say? I've got a touch of the Oprah in me.

I have friends who are not like me or Oprah. They go to bed at 8:30 p.m. They've never watched Dexter. They jog five kilometres in the morning while I'm still drooling into my buckwheat pillow. I have a forty-six-year-old friend who has six-pack abs and weighs only 138 pounds, lighter than he was in high school. The man is despica-ble. He swims every day, and sometime even at lunch. Even at lunch, I tell you! He is doing laps while I circle KFC with my car window open. Breathe in. Breathe out.

I don't pretend to understand the lives of the so-called perfect people. Their smiles are all shiny white and they look impossibly good at the beach. I don't know how they do it. I don't want to know either. I have yellow teeth and a superb paunch. What am I going to do? Am I going to get all military on myself and go to one of those boot camps? Nope. Will I ever go to hot yoga? You first, Oprah. I want to see you in sweat-stained Lululemon.

Listen, I'm curious about many things, but one of the things I am really tired of is my dissatisfaction with myself. Gee willickers, I'm all I have. Why poke yourself in the eye with a pogo stick? Why beat yourself about the head with a Toblerone? I'd rather pull up a chair, unpinch my bag of Oreos, and watch Ellen.

I Golf Therefore
I Forget

Thirteen years ago we went to Maui for a twenty-one day vacation. It took me about twenty days to finally relax. My wife says that relaxation is my personal demon. To relax does not come easily for me. There is simply too much to worry about.

On day twenty of our Maui vacation, I experienced a sense of peace that can only come from twenty days of sheer restlessness. I'd put 2000 miles on our poor rental car and completed three laps around the volcanic island. In twenty days I'd read every half decent novel published that year — two or three a day. We'd also seen every movie, snorkeled at all the reefs, and visited nearly every budget restaurant, cafe, and historic sight.

"What's next?" asked my wife. I sat on the hotel bed flipping between Hawaii Five-O and Magnum PI.

"Let's find the island's power source, protest for alternatives like wind or biofuel, and then let's look for the poor people, preferably poor native people ..."

"Huh? You want to what?!"

"I guess I don't do well on islands," I replied. "Especially those colonized by odiferous Europeans and voracious wild pigs."

"You're a nut ball!" she said. "You need a hobby. Don't spoil this vacation by searching for diesel generators and indigenous poverty. They hide the unsightly generators and poor. Just like at home."

"Yeah, okay, dear."

"Don't 'dear' me. Hawaii is where any responsible person comes to vacation. It's already spoiled, colonized, and paved over, okay? This is the highly travelled, highly sustainable path. We're consciously not exploring new ground or ruining things that haven't already been thoroughly ruined, okay?"

"Yeah okay," I replied.

Thirteen years later, my wife reports that power generation on Maui is more sustainable, and I haven't come any closer to solving my relaxation/worry woes. There are so many obstacles that prevent me from relaxing.

The first one is my addiction to work-related email. The second one is the immense amount of useless shopping available on the Internet. The third one is the multi-channel television universe and my Olympian talent for being able to watch the same hockey highlight seventeen times. The fourth one is the condition of our beautiful and desperate world.

No biggie, right?

In light of these nearly insurmountable obstacles, I've concluded that I must find a hobby that is 1) a significant waste of time; 2) takes place in the great outdoors; 3) involves caloric expenditure; 4) accomplishes little or nothing; and 5) will cause me to be uplifted and rejuvenated. I've consulted all the experts; there are only two things I can do: take up golf or have an affair.

Having an affair is probably not the best of ideas. They tend to induce a lot of showering and require well-conditioned abdominal muscles. Affairs make you feel guilty no matter how enlightened you think you are, and they require the kind of body that looks good naked.

The great thing about golf is that you are expressly forbidden to play it naked. The Greeks, who played their sports naked, never anticipated how a naked John Daly might look while squatting down for a lag putt. Can you picture it now?

So golf it is!

Unlike sex, golf rewards sub par performance and may be the quintessential perfect waste of time. After 18 holes you feel relaxed, even though you have spent roughly four hours doing nothing about world hunger, child poverty, economic productivity, or any of the million others things you could be doing in your spare time.

Certainly, charity golf is an absolutely perfect waste of time, but even charity golf comes with a hefty price tag. Golf membership ranges from $1800 to $17,000 in the valley, then you've got to get a set of cast or forged irons that range from $200 to $1500. A Sasquatch driver can run you $400. A tour-proven Odyssey putter at least $150. A golf bag (Bag Boy), golf towel (Burberry), golf shirt (J. Lindberg), golf belt (Nike), golf umbrella (Mizuno), golf tees (Stinger), golf glove (TaylorMade), golf wedges (KZG), golf shoes (Adidas), and utility clubs (Adams) will set you back a cool grand. Golf balls, if you must know, aren't cheap either.

The Pro V1 golf ball costs you six bucks every time you splash into that perfectly-placed water hazard. Ask any golfer, once you splash a Pro V1, the natural thing to do is hit it in the water over and over again until someone cuffs you upside the head.

Titleist, the company that makes this ball, has convinced golfers that it is the Holy Grail. What do you get for your six bucks? Apparently, this ball adds length to your game, spins like crazy on your forged wedges, and putts like a baby's bottom. If you sleep with the ball under your pillow, it will get rid of the skin tags on your neck and thwart constipation. No, really.

Every year there is some wacky golf technology that everybody falls hook, line, and sinker for. This summer, it was square-headed drivers. This spring, it was the stack and tilt technique used by Mike Weir to revamp his swing and recover from lower back woes. Next year, someone will come up with a crazy new idea and golfers will be momentarily mesmerized.

What will be the next huge thing? Two words: yoga golf. You heard it here.

The wonderful thing about golf is that even though it is barely affordable, even though it is a poor excuse for exercise, and even though most golf courses are not exactly great for the environment (i.e., water use), golf is actually kind of boring and that is a good thing.

Golf is pleasant. That's its key strength. It's far from particularly thrilling or climactic. You get a pleasant walk with a few pals. You are nearly always pleasantly hungry at the end of it. Best of all, you forget a lot of things when you're playing golf.

For four hours you forget that we have no solutions for homelessness. We have no solutions for our broken heath and education systems. You forget that we have no solutions for our inadequate system of transnational, national, provincial, and regional governance. We have no effective ideas for solving child poverty, terrorism, Afghanistan, AIDS, bird flu, acid rain, rain forest depletion, global warming, or whom to support in the next election.

That's why golf is so great. It's so damn straightforward. You hit the ball. You walk. You hit the ball. You look for the ball. You hit the ball. Splash. You hit another. You hear the metallic CRACK of a six-dollar ball against the four hundred dollar face of a metal wood. You duck. You duck again.

Nothing could be simpler in these complex times.

From Good to Great

"Good is the enemy of great." – VOLTAIRE

A few years ago, Tiger Woods shocked the sporting world by completely rebuilding his already excellent golf swing. He promptly returned to golf better than ever. Not long ago, Steve Jobs took his computer company into the world of consumer electronics and, against all advice, launched the iPod. He reinvented his company and changed the future of music and video.

Whether you're talking about the reinvention of entrepreneurs like Jobs or athletes like Michael Jordan (who returned from retirement to re-conquer his sport), reinvention is a common theme in the understanding of human expertise.

Reinvention is also a theme in the spiritual realm. Many religious traditions speak of being born again. Christianity distinguishes itself from other traditions with its focus of transcending the ego and entering a new consciousness. Easter is the time when many Christians reflect on the state of their personal transcendence.

Spring can make us feel part of the cycle of life where the old becomes new again, or it can remind us that the natural cycle (birth, life, and death) can be transcended. Organizations throughout the world are greeting an economic equation that is unprecedented in its complexity and ambiguity. Some of us are waiting, locked in a combination of fear and uncertainty.

Others are seeking greatness.

Jim Collins noted (along with Voltaire in 1764) that "good is the enemy of great." In other words, people and organizations who believe they are good remain locked in a status quo that offers little incentive to change, let alone attain greatness.

Is good really the "enemy" of great? At first glance, we may believe that greatness evolves from goodness like steps up a ladder. We like to think that if we try, train, and persevere we will step across the threshold and reach greatness. So how, then, can good be the "enemy" of great?

Isn't "enemy" just a dramatic way of saying that good and great do not exist in the same continuum, but actually oppose one another? How is a good school, hospital, city, the enemy of a great school, hospital, city? If I am a good father, then how is my goodness the enemy of greatness?

One of the chief complaints about being good at anything is the complacency it develops. "I'm good," you say to yourself, "I deserve a pat on the back, not a kick in the backside." Complacency says that good is good enough. It stops you from striving; it asks you to rest on your laurels. Ask any financial institution about the dangers of complacency.

Complacency has an enabling cousin named "entitlement." "Hey, give me a cotton-pickin' break," you say to yourself. "I deserve credit for how great I was last week, last year, last decade." The attitude of entitlement is almost always about the power of the ego; it's about hanging onto a glorified golden past when you were truly appreciated and the spoils were yours to keep.

The willful and fanciful distortion of history may be quite common among all of us who used to be good at something. "The older I get, the better I used to be," the saying goes.

"I'm almost there," you say to yourself. "If I wanted, I could be at the pinnacle of achievement if it weren't for the darn market, my bum knee, the price of petroleum, or my 'fill-in-the-bank' hard luck story." Excuses have a way of feeding self-talk that distorts the past, making it even harder to break the tyranny of "good enough."

Those who aspire to greatness face the insecurity, risk, and vulnerability that a reality-based assessment might provide. If we compare ourselves to ourselves, it's easy to look good, but things change when you choose tough measures that force you to face reality. There may be an awful feeling when you compare yourself against the best and examine the facts: you may feel insecure or inspired.

What the heck is greatness anyway? Once you hit the mark, is someone going to slap a medal on your chest? Is there some recognition that will grant you enduring greatness?

Greatness is probably not a destination, a mountain to be conquered, or a medal to be bestowed. It is, on the contrary, the ordinary accumulation of practicing the extra-ordinary. Greatness is about becoming new. It is a reinvention. Transcendence. A constant journey.

What kind of greatness do you want?

Well, if I could be great at anything, it would be in the quality of love I give. My love is often lazy, ego-driven, shallow, fleeting. I also understand now, more than ever, how much I fear the vulnerability that accompanies emotional risk.

My journey, if I can handle it, is the reinvention of love, of learning the difference between offering good love and offering great love. My growth will be a function of an ability to live in the moment when the self disappears into ... connectedness.

In the best of these moments, I feel surrounded by the embrace of my parents. I recall the caresses of friends and family. I surrender to the patience and wisdom of all who have supported, trained, and scolded me. Then I dare myself to make the leap, to love in a way that breaks through the bustle of work, the preoccupation with fear, and this desperate inability to hear the beating heart of others.

The Aspirational World

"It's not having what you want. It's wanting what you've got."
"If it makes you happy, then why the hell are you so sad?"
— SHERYL CROW

When I was a kid growing up in the seventies, I tried with all my might, not to be hypnotized by the bras and girdles in the Christmas catalogue. Each person in my family went through the catalogue in his or her own way. It was as if the contents represented the universe of choice to us, the universe of what you could buy and who you could be. Today, of course, the old Eaton's or Sears catalogues are often thought of as quaint precursors to the over-consumption that characterizes nearly all our problems. These catalogues showed Canadians a view of normality; the images, however flawed, mirrored our humble material expectations and modest dreams. It wasn't very long ago, at least in my mind, when tall white snowmobile boots were the epitome of Canadian luxury and high fashion. When I was eleven, I could only dream of owning a pair.

What replaced these catalogues? Magazines and television shows that told us, just like the catalogues did, what was normal, what was expected, and what was within reach. Magazines for women promoted not just things you could do with a can of mushroom soup, but the idea that the so-called "home-maker" needed to be emancipated from the chains of domesticity and discrimination. Throughout the seventies, as women exchanged their homes for the workplace, we saw images of liberation and financial confidence reflected in fashion, décor, and food magazines.

Men, too, began to see themselves and their aspirations reflected
in magazines. Whether it was woodworking, fishing, cars, sports, or
something more risqué, men soon discovered that whatever the interest, there was more than just *Popular Mechanics* available. Most
of us, as we scoured these new, huge, magazine racks in the seventies and eighties, knew that sooner or later we would find values,
images, and, most importantly, a set of specific purchases, like those
beautiful furniture-making tools or a collection of fly rods, that would
create in us a sense of identity.

Television shows in the seventies which espoused a particularly traditional view of middle class expectations such as Happy
Days, The Waltons, and Little House on the Prairie, to name a few,
gave way to shows that ten years later prefigured our obsession with
wealth: Dallas, Magnum PI, and The Cosby Show. Today, in shows
like Beverly Hills 90210 and Desperate Housewives, we are enter-
tained not just by the storylines, but by the upscale images: luxury
cars, designer fashions, and high-end interior décor.

The nineties didn't just bring us cleavage and greed; it brought
a new set of magazines that were to influence us in ways that we
could not expect. These magazines were off-shoots of familiar home
decorating magazines, but with an added injection of celebrity and
allure. The magazine industry soon partnered with Hollywood so
that sales in both would rise. Add a star to the cover of *InStyle* or
Architectural Digest and sales boomed.

This new alliance between magazines, style, and celebrity created our zeitgeist of entertainment and consumerism. In the seventies, you might have read a magazine and wanted a new haircut. In
the eighties, you might have wished for a sports car to accompany
the thumping soundtrack of your life. In the nineties, celebrities began sharing their homes, their furniture, their kitchens, their reci-
pes, and the aesthetic of wealth became what it is now — a nearly
unconscious, middle-class, sense of expectation and entitlement.
Martha Stewart and Oprah Winfrey became more than arbiters of
style — they told us what to eat, how to dress, what to read, and,
more importantly, what we deserved.

The result of all this cross-marketing is that we feel entitled to live the life reflected in our magazines and screens. We want to live like stars; this aspiration was easily responded to by a financial industry more than willing to provide the right products, such as low-interest loans, loyalty credit cards, and 40-year mortgages, so that we could indulge in the life of our dreams before we had the means.

Instead of flipping through a catalogue at Christmas hoping to find that perfect robe for mom, or that musky soap on the rope for dad, we spend in five and ten thousand dollar blocks. $5K for that Mexican cruise or trip to Disneyland. $5K for that gleaming appliance with professional chef features. $5K for that home theatre. $10K for that spa. And, as we all know, rarely are these purchases paid for in cash. Aspirational cross-marketing continues to bombard us in our daily lives. We are told that we are what we buy and that success is marked by our addresses and possessions. In the Okanagan, we are making the transition to a resort economy; we must now live the resort lifestyle. The "must haves" in a resort are many: carbon fibre bikes, kayaks, hard top convertibles, dream kitchens, rippling buns and abs, and the erasure of the poor.

The entertainment industry is dominated by the art and science of product placement. Virtually nothing you see on the screen is there by accident. James Bond's latest vehicle is an easy pick, but the billboards that form the backdrop of the action scenes have been carefully monetized. Video game manufacturers, movie producers, and commercial directors spend just as much time producing a soundtrack for their products as they do developing their products, so that revenue streams and cross-marketing channels can be thoroughly integrated by radio, Internet, movies, magazines, books, and television.

The result of all this is supposed to be a high standard of living generated by a booming consumer economy encased in a culture of expenditure. The biggest expenditure of all, the dwelling we live in, represents the showcase of our identities. We are judged by where we live, how big our kitchen islands are, and how seamlessly we have incorporated the aesthetic borrowed from our coffee table magazines. It is no wonder that the world-wide crash we see in the financial markets originated in the housing sector where buyers' eyes were larger than their bank accounts.

Even the green movement, ostensibly about using less carbon-based energy and protecting our precious natural resources, has been fueled by celebrity, fashion, and materialism. We want to be green, but only because it is cool, fashionable, and part of the never-ending campaign to keep up with one's neighbours.

When I was a boy, we were not immune to consumerism. We said good night to each other, just like on The Waltons. My mother made a dessert from lemon Jello and cream cheese from a recipe found in the back of *Chatelaine*. I dreamed of shooting like Bobby Hull, as well as using the same skates, stick, and Bic pen he endorsed. Canada was a different place, a more innocent, simple, and less diverse place. It was Tacks or Supremes, Ford or Chevy, Lee or Levi, Chinese or Japanese. We didn't question the size of our kitchens, worry that our homes didn't have enough wow factor, or factor in a diverse and complicated world where not everybody wants what we want.

Nostalgia won't heal us now, especially as our real estate and investment portfolios dip. The entertainment capital of the world is sinking under the weight of its chief marketing tool — happiness through consumption. The great idyllic American Dream that drove the aspirations of the entire world is less about reaching your potential as a human being than living large and paying for it later. Later, I suppose, is now.

Life and Taxes

How would you like to take home your entire paycheque? Absolutely no taxes from the province or Ottawa. Nothing taken off. Your gross pay would be your net take-home pay. How would you like that? How would that be?

How would we fund our governments then? Well, instead of taxing at the source, we would create a consumption tax — one tax for everyone on everything you consume. No tax breaks except for the poor.

This tax plan sounds crazy, doesn't it? Yeah, okay, I admit it does, but there has been a lot of research done into it.

The consumption tax idea is part of the platform supported by Republican presidential candidate Governor Mike Huckabee, among many others. While I may not agree with all aspects of Huckabee's platform, I can't help but love the idea of keeping as much of my paycheque as possible.

A consumption tax has been explored by economists as a much fairer alternative to a flat tax which can create inequities. A consumption tax is an intriguing idea because it is based upon how much you buy and consume, not how much you make. The more you consume, the more tax you pay.

As you know, we currently buy our goods and services with hard-earned, after-tax earnings. And, of course, did you know that the goods and services we buy already have built-in taxes such as hidden manufacturing taxes? So a consumption tax would conceivably remove all those invisible taxes, stop us from paying taxes two or more times, and, in the long run, probably make things cheaper.

Experts suggest that if the United States were to adopt this admittedly radical idea, the consumption tax would be around 23 percent in order to support the current government budget levels. That may sound really high, but remember you get to keep your whole darn paycheque.

I am not saying the consumption tax will solve all our problems, but it is intriguing to think about how this idea might impact our consumer society, where nearly every human experience seems designed to get us to consume and then consume some more.

In Brazil, certain cities are banning all outdoor advertising. You can walk to the park without being bombarded by messages urging you to consume. In fact, activists the world over are becoming more and more interested in creating social and cultural spaces that aren't impacted by branding and marketing.

Wouldn't it be great to live a day, an hour, a minute without being bombarded by branding and persuasion?

I think it's pretty hard to manage a space that isn't impacted by advertising. I am not just talking about corporate sponsorship in urinals and the renaming of our publicly-funded institutions. Business is not the enemy; all of us, if we stop and think about it, know we can all do a better job preserving the sanctity of what advertisers call our "mind space."

The green movement is a big part of the equation, and it has moved forward with great pace, but there is still an important disconnect on one contradiction. A green world and one dominated by consumption are not compatible. It is not good enough to simply fill our dumps with environmentally friendly products. We have to not just start consuming different products, but learn to stop buying things in order to create identity.

Are you a BMW or are you a Lexus? That's the question advertisers want you to answer. The real question is, why allow branding to determine what you think of yourself. Am I a sophisticated cool guy just because I have brie and imported beer in my fridge? Am I a low-class bunion just because I eat nachos in front of American Idol?

Are we what we consume? That's the message we've heard since forever.

I have always been cynical about tax reform. It's not that I don't believe in tax incentives. Yes, they work. But I do think that we have been very shy about being more innovative about taxation. I think it's time we came up with some new ideas on how we fund our government. I think it's time to ask ourselves the big question: Are we happy with this way of life?

Some economists believe that we must maximize our resources and continually grow our profits. Now there is a new chorus of economists who have realized that maximizing growth is simply not sustainable. In the end, we will have no fish, no trees, no oil, and no people to enjoy the profits.

Isn't it time for a different model? Some boldly say a different model of happiness or social satisfaction is needed. Perhaps happiness is not an SUV, a place at the ski hill, or out-doing your neighbour's media room. While we cannot deny the benefit of a materially comfortable life, we don't seem to know what else to do after we've retired from the rink or the oil field than blast around the lake in a really loud speed boat.

Is that living? Is that the epitome?

By taxing consumption and allowing us to keep our entire paycheque, we may learn to spend our pennies differently.

I know what I would do if I got to keep my entire paycheque. At first, I'd go crazy with temptation. Then I'd sit down and ask myself the age-old questions: What do I really want? What makes my life meaningful? How do I want to be remembered?

If we ever got a consumption tax, I'd consume less so that I could work exactly half as much. Then I'd sit down with my family and say, "What do we want to do? Where do we want to go? What kind of family do we want to be?"

Lyla from New Brunswick

I met three grade four students in an urban elementary school in Saint John, New Brunswick. This was a very successful elementary school with an impressive 100% high school graduation rate, but it was afflicted by generational poverty.

The principal informed me in the staff room that the majority of parents did not own a home or a vehicle. Through corporate and community support, the children in the school were provided with a daily hot lunch. Each student also had a community reading buddy who visited regularly.

The classroom was well-equipped with circular tables, up-to-date technology, and comfortable chairs. I noticed a fancy Smart Board attached to the Internet, so I showed the children a Google map of Canada. I asked Allen to locate the Okanagan. He struggled, but after a few moments, carefully pointed it out. Then I expanded the map to include the entire world.

"If you could go anywhere, anywhere you want, where would you go?" I asked.

Red-haired Roberta scrunched up her face. Tall Lyla put her chin in her hands. Allen raised his hand and said, "Edmonton. Because my grampa works there."

"Me, I'd like to go to Paris," said Roberta.

"Why do you want to visit Paris?"

"'Cause it's real far." The kids laughed.

Lyla put her hand up finally. "So, where would you like to go, Lyla?"

"Moncton."

"Lyla, Moncton is only a few hours away. You can pick any place in the entire world."

"Moncton. I was there when I was small so I don't remember it."

When I asked the principal about Lyla afterward, she told me that the tall girl had struggled at home and at school.

"Why Moncton?" I asked. "It's only 155 km away."

"It may be a lifetime away for Lyla," the principal said. "Her world may be pretty limited."

I think about Lyla from New Brunswick quite often. I remember holding her hand on the way to our hot lunch. We sat huddled together chatting. We ate chicken, mashed potatoes, and gravy. I remember talking about my own little girl who is nearly the same age. We might have talked about books and dreams and far away places, but we didn't. We drank our cold milk, made little indentations in our potatoes for gravy, and we grinned a lot about nothing. This girl's smile was so beautiful and open. For some reason, she brings tears to my eyes.

In Moncton, a few days later, my group ate dinner with the Lieutenant Governor of New Brunswick and his partner who was a theatre professor who produced locally developed plays written in French. I talked about Lyla because I couldn't get her off my mind.

"Her ambition was very modest," the Lieutenant Governor said. "What can we do to help broaden her horizons?"

"Aren't all of us somehow limited by our worldview?" said the drama professor. "Our worldview is the product of our upbringing, our education, but most of all it is limited by our own imaginations."

"Ah, you are talking about the role of art," said the erudite Lieutenant Governor.

Art remains a controversial subject. Some view art as essentially useless, especially when governments spend money supporting public art or emerging artists. Others view art as essentially the core of our economic and social life, linking art to design, creativity, innovation, and values.

The culture that we live in, the one that establishes our values and beliefs, is derived from the imaginations of our creative class which includes our novelists, painters, directors, architects, musicians, and many other kinds of creative people.

Businesses, too, prize the employee with the ability to hone new ideas into marketable products and services. Those who question the impact of art and artists on our culture generally hold a limited worldview concerning the transformative power of art.

When I view myself as an artist, I realize how much I am being held back by my own worldview. The way I write, the way I think, the way I imagine — in a strange way, I am no different than Lyla from New Brunswick.

I cannot see beyond Moncton in so many ways. When I push the boundaries of my creativity, I realize how difficult it is to see with fresh eyes, and I treasure and value the artist even more.

For example, there is an artist (Elizabeth Demaray) who has designed and manufactured "Hand-Up," a plastic shell, for hermit crabs to use as prefab homes. This ecological art not only raises awareness about the environmental pressures facing hermit crabs who can't find housing, but also demonstrates how art can be life-saving and life-affirming.

There are many visual artists who find themselves resisting traditional ideas of what art means; artists like Robert Smithson (whose earthworks I find shockingly interesting) don't show their work in galleries because galleries can't hold a work like Spiral Jetty which was built on Rozel Point in Great Salt Lake, Utah.

Some artists do not use existing materials, so they spend years devising special fabrications and technologies. Others use only found materials. Some create art out of snow or ice, or even the voices of starlings, reminding us of the power and beauty of nature. These artists challenge the frontiers of our expectations about the value of art which invites the reflective person to re-think, re-imagine, and re-experience the world.

Although I am a writer and choose to make my contribution with words, I cannot over-estimate what I have gained from confronting the world of experimental, conceptual, and environmental art. The Olympic Sculpture Park in Seattle, for example, has changed the way I see the relationship between art and urbanity. Proving that a gallery is not the only place to discover art, the Olympic Sculpture Park is placed in a beautiful outdoor space that was once industrial land.

Lyla from New Brunswick transformed my own worldview about the nature of generational poverty. She taught me to think of my own poverty, which is, of course, nothing like hers. My own poverty is one that is connected to my worldview.

A worldview is shaped by our experiences, learning, travel, and relationships. If your worldview is not constantly shifting, adapting, and growing then it can be linked to a kind of creative dormancy. To see yourself and the world anew should be our constant challenge.

Art teaches us not to frame others by our own experience. Art inspires us to challenge the way we experience life. Art humbles us, shakes our foundations, and tells us that the most significant journey we ever take is the one that points us to a place we've never been.

Lyla, why do you really want to go Moncton? I asked her at the end of our time together.

"Because I was born there," she said.

STAN CHUNG

The Burden of Choice

"Freedom of choice is essential to self-respect, public participation, mobility, and nourishment, but not all choice enhances freedom. Increased choice among goods and services may contribute little or nothing to the kind of freedom that counts. Indeed, it may impair freedom by taking time and energy we'd be better off devoting to other matters."
— BARRY SCHWARTZ

We march out of the shower and hop one-footed into the day. Make-up is applied while driving. The digital clock hustles children into morning panic.

Where are we going with such speed?

My friend Doug tells me they walk fast on the sidewalks in Paris. Even in the leisurely Okanagan, some of us wake before dawn to fret over the eastern stock exchanges.

Late at night I hear motorcycles racing. Ambulance lights twinkle across the lake. Some child is trying not to dream about the near-miss at the crosswalk. We tap our heels in the coffee lineup or rap our fingers while waiting for a web page to load. Rush, rush, rush. No time to spare. All the choices in the world, all the power of technology, all the freedom a democratic society can offer — and so much disillusionment.

Why are there 246 kinds of shampoo? Why is buying a toothbrush an act of agony?

Our heart rates rise. Our blood pressure boils. Our caffeinated identities pulse to twice the size. It's no wonder we're stressed out.

We want the best out of life, but selection takes so much effort.

The pace of modernity erases the biological rhythm of life. Did you know that it is summer now? It scarcely registers unless we are forced to stop and take notice.

Look at the June sky. Feel the musty heat. Smell the warm wind. Do you really need to drive around town looking for the best this and the cheapest that?

And even when I sit still and try to focus, my mind wanders. Why?

Sit still. Slow down. Take it easy. Step aside. Take a breath. Cool down. Check out. Hold your breath. Listen. Hear. Swallow. Breathe again.

Breathing exercises can help you slow down and experience a quiet mind and body. I practice breathing all the time, but it's tough to get good at something so seemingly natural. Breathing from deep inside your belly takes skill. Try taking ten deep breaths and, if you're anything like me, before you get to the count of five, your mind will go skittering away. I need new tires. The vacuum needs a filter. The line of credit is rising. Our countertops suck.

Why is it so hard to quiet the mind?

Sometimes my children ask me about the pace of life.

"Dad, why are you always rushing? Why are you so busy?" I shrug my shoulders. "Well ... because I have no choice."

Really?

A few years ago, I read a book on discovering one's strengths and discovered I was a "Maximizer." That made me feel kind of good. I am one of those people who like to get the best out of my choices. I can't help it.

I've only recently figured out that my strength has its dark side. It turns out that I need help figuring out what choices are worth maximizing and what choices I should just forget about.

Do I really need to spend three hours on the Internet figuring out which all-season tires have the best wear rating to price ratio? How much research on stainless steel rice pots can one person do?

If I'm not careful, I can be an indiscriminate maximizer. If I let myself, I will analyze things that aren't worth the time and effort.

Maybe maximizing is going to kill me. Kryptonite for a maximizer is to discover too many choices. People like me love choices, want choices, but find it hard to admit that choices can sometimes paralyze and turn us into idiots.

If you only knew how much time I spend thinking about tennis racquet string, tennis racquet string tension, and tennis racquet string gauge. Do you know I have two types of string in my racquet at two different tensions, each string with a unique gauge, brand, and colour? Do I need hospitalization?

Did you know freedom could be so restrictive? Hey, you can do anything, any time, so it's no wonder people rush around not knowing what matters and what doesn't.

What should we do? Much maximizing activity is crazy. It's like driving around all day to save two cents a litre on gas. The endless travelling, the endless researching, the endless choosing — it's helping us go nowhere incredibly fast.

Researchers tell us to consciously limit our choices. New research in behavioural economics, choice architecture, and positive psychology are telling us that having more choices doesn't necessarily make you happier.

In fact, you might be better off learning how to constrain your freedom. Make a budget. Give yourself some limits. Make a line you will not cross. Make a choice to limit your choices. Stop sweating the details of the little stuff.

Remember when you were a kid and you went to your mother and begged for something to do?

"Mom, I'm so bored. What can I do? There's nothing to do."

"You have two choices, kid. You can go outside or you can go outside."

"Mom!"

Life was simple in the good old days. The choices were perfect.

What are the odds that all the best friends I had as a kid just happened to be the kid next door? What magical power was intervening for me? Or was it something else?

Limit your choices. Choose the right things to maximize. Sometimes you don't need the very best. Sometimes good enough is just perfect. Put down the mouse, flick off the TV, lay down this newspaper, take a deep breath, and make your freedom really count.

STAN CHUNG

Gretel in Whistler

"Am I alone? Spies
hiss in the stillness, Hansel,
we are there still and it is real, real,
that black forest and the fire in earnest."
— LOUISE GLUCK

When she rolls out of her bed in the morning, my sister lies still and checks for pain. Her rheumatoid arthritis can be disabling, but she has kept the autoimmune disease at bay through exercise and lifestyle.

It's hard to know exactly what she means by lifestyle.

She walks downstairs to her piano studio where she has made a small bed for me. I've slept nearly ten hours which is a lot more than I usually get, but I can barely get up to check my work phone for messages.

You ready? She asks. Okay. I don't know if I'm ready to go for a long walk. Visiting my sister is like going on vacation and the first thing that always hits me is how tired I am. From her basement window, I can see snow-covered peaks and the circular shape of a cirque.

How long are you going to be? She asks.

Three minutes, I say quickly.

My sister lives in Whistler, a ski resort two hours north of Vancouver. She has lived there most of her adult life with her husband, two teenage boys, and doodle dog who refuses to come to me. Like most people, she considers her life pretty average, despite her 60-student, piano studio and design consulting business.

Hardly, I say to myself.

We jump into her station wagon with heated steering wheel and leather upholstery. We drive to a little known area away from the Olympic tourists. There are remnants of old cabins and an old mill from the days when Whistler was a yet undeveloped fishing camp. We meet up with her friend Heather who holds a golden retriever and a cup of coffee. There are little plastic bags tied like flowers to the dog leash.

Where do you live? she asks.

I tell her and we are off on a fast-paced walk on the valley trail, an iconic series of trails that my sister helped design when she worked as a landscape architect and planner for the resort municipality.

Look at the sky, she exclaims. Heather looks great for fifty. She skis, looks after her teens, plays squash, and seems to be the kind of stunning practical woman my sister has become.

I didn't know what to say to women without careers before, my sister said on the way to Heather's gorgeous lakeside place.

My sister explains that it is a significant family achievement to position someone who can play the role of family caregiver without being forced into the workplace.

Although I know women who find being at home, difficult and still others who seem to mainly shop and attend yoga classes, I don't say anything.

I don't miss the job, says my sister who walks her dog every morning as if it were the most important thing a person could do. Maybe it is, I wonder.

Look at that sky, says Heather again. We might have to head up and gets some runs in. What a life, I say to myself. If I had this kind of time, what would get me up in the morning? Would I look as good as these two? Do I even like myself enough to care for myself in this way?

The walk feels so good.

It is February and the skies have cleared. Even though the 2010 Olympics are on, with the women's downhill being held on the mountain today, the locals know where to ski and find solace even under the noses of fifty thousand visitors.

I can barely keep pace with the women and their dogs. They chat amiably, but they are moving fast. They point out changes in the landscape. The village is now investing in public art. There is a new train station on Nita Lake. Heather's husband is a custom builder. My sister's husband is a city manager.

My sister is about five foot four. She is three inches taller than our mother. She is the type of woman who communicates clearly with people. Some would call her direct.

When we were very young, our parents left us for a year in Korea while they went to Canada. We lived with our grandmother in Seoul. I remember the newspaper in the outhouse. My sister was about two years old. I was nearly four. There is a black and white photograph of me holding her hand. It is the Korean way to be told repeatedly to take care of your younger siblings.

I wonder now what I told her when our parents left. I wonder, too, what I told her when we met our parents again in Canada. We didn't recognize them. I even asked for proof, which made my mother cry. They were strangers to us. We were Hansel and Gretel. To be abandoned and then adopted by strangers. She didn't talk for the longest time.

Her only constant was me. My only constant was her. My sister and I are one.

When she was in grade five, my sister sprained her ankle at the ski hill. She held up pretty well. She was carried onto the school bus where I waited for her. I hid because I didn't want to show her that I was sobbing. I was supposed to take care of her, and I had failed.

I have grown up to be a caretaker kind of person, but I am now aware that my sister has always considered this trait a bit of a weakness. Before I married, she told me that she wanted me to find someone to protect me. I listened to this advice because before then I had no idea that my sister saw how foolish I really was.

You're not like me, she says to me on the trail under the icy blue sky. You don't know how not to care.

When you watch your sister grow up, you like to think that you're partially responsible for your sister's successes. I grew up trying to entertain her, make her giggle, and get her to act more like a brother.

I tried to teach her how to box, how to fish, how to wrestle, how to play tennis, and, when we were older, how to allow me to chase her female friends. She put up with her older brother's cavalier interests. She put up with me trying to pretend that I had rescued her.

One of the biggest moments of my life was when my sister's husband left her. She doesn't know that I constantly worried that he wouldn't come back. I really missed him, but I knew it wasn't up to me to figure out how to save a young marriage.

It took my sister months of therapy and soul-searching to travel across the country to Nova Scotia to get her husband back – to feel what it is to apologize from the deepest part of you – and to know what it means to rescue love from heartbreak. Only that little girl in the photograph would know.

I'm not the smartest guy in the world when it comes to love, marriage, and relationships, but my kid sister taught me a lesson when she told me nearly seventeen years ago that her husband was coming back home. She told me that they were going to build a family from a foundation of rescued love, Gretel's love that was to be forged from mistakes and humility and forgiveness.

When I go to Whistler, I am treated to an insider's view of the spectacular jewel that has admirably hosted the 2010 Olympics. But most of all, I am treated to the company of my sister and brother-in-law who continually teach me not to fear the fire and the black forest.

Waiting for D-day

Mary and Dave are getting divorced after twenty-five years of marriage. My question is "what's the rush?" Why did they wait twenty-five years?

I don't want to get into specifics here, like Dave's billion dollar putter collection or Mary's aspiration to sell her art at the next craft show. I don't want to tell you that Dave's goal in life is to upgrade his home theatre and that Mary's goal is to find herself, especially far away from Dave.

I don't want to tell you these details because one of the first things you learn in adult life is that the only relationship you can judge is your own.

Some people scrap like dogs and cats and still manage to stay together; on the other hand, a quiet argument about nothing can break a couple into two with nothing left but legal bills.

Relationships are tricky things. It's easy to lapse into tired formulas like "it's all about the money" or "it's all about listening" or "it's all about getting an extremely unattractive but effective housekeeper, secretary, or gardener."

Despite his sports car, golf membership, and HD plasma screen, Dave is a pretty bitter fellow. He says he had no early warning that Mary was unhappy. He thought their relationship was peachy keen. "Maybe I would have tried to change, but I didn't know what she was looking for. I still don't."

Mary says that she's been biding her time, waiting for a chance to escape. She was tired of the endless grind of her role. She not only works, but she looks after the household. "The shopping, cooking, cleaning, care-taking, keeping my body acceptable – isn't there more to life than back-stopping a man? I need time for me."

"Time for you?" shouts Dave. "Have you been in prison for twenty-five years? We've got a nice house, great friends, and a place at the ski hill. I didn't realize you were suffering so much."

"You don't get it," replies Mary. "You do whatever you want. Marriage is about male privilege. I'm tired of picking up your damn socks."

How can both people believe they are getting the short end of the stick? Can these mid-life divorces be about both a woman's desire for self-actualization and a man's shock that financial security does not a marriage make?

"Nobody bothered to tell me that the rules had changed," says Dave. "Nobody told me that women have a buffet of choices and that all men get is combat duty. We work. Then we die. That's it."

"Let me be perfectly honest," says Mary, "I want to live life in a meaningful way. I want to be fully alive. I want to enjoy all that life has to offer. I'm not interested in being someone's wife."

"Nobody told me that 'wife' was a nasty four-letter word," says Dave.

It's nothing new to say that men and women can fundamentally misunderstand each other's needs, but it may be interesting to begin mapping out a new definition for marriage, especially if marriage is to survive beyond children and mortgages and sleek waistlines.

Is it any surprise to you that, according to Sarah Hampson's recent piece in the *Globe and Mail*, the majority of divorces above the age of forty are initiated by women?

Is it any surprise to you that marriage is one factor that statisticians say has been proven to increase our lifespan? Just as we spurn it, we discover that marriage is the best thing for us.

"I'd rather have a short happy life than a long miserable one," quips Mary.

"That can be arranged, honey."

As more and more people separate, choose to live alone, or decide not to be married in the first place, marriage becomes the exception not the norm.

Traditional gender roles have changed but many mid-life couples are still confused because they don't know what the new rules are. What does he do? What does she do? Who decides about the position of the toilet seat? How do we find the right balance between our own needs and the needs of our partner?

Baby-boomers are not only facing retirement surrounded by issues such as the "meaning of my life" and the "legacy of my life," but they also have to pay for the "darn good life," and we all know "life" ain't cheap.

Down-sizing is no longer a top priority for so-called empty nesters. Making your success obvious has moved with a bullet to number one. Thus, the custom wine cellar business is booming. Luxury automobiles are selling like hotcakes. (The list of luxury items that were once optional and that have now become middle-class mandatory is endless.)

Expectations concerning retirement have changed, too. No longer do we want to pay off our mortgages while we save for retirement. No, we want it ALL.

And we want it NOW. Every day the luxo-monoculture slaps us in the face like our friend's spanking new convertible, or whatever else your friend has that you don't have, and it cannot help but make us incredibly dis-satisfied with our lives.

Who has the power to resist the pressure to make our consumption so conspicuous?

"We're in debt up to our eyeballs because Mary wanted the big rancher with the lake view," says Dave. "You just couldn't stop competing with your friends, could you? You wanted a bigger stove, fancier countertops, a killer powder room."

"Yeah? Who bought the turbo, the saltwater pool, the steam shower, the electronics? Nobody twisted your arm, Dave. We both bought into the lifestyle of impatience."

"And now it's not good enough for you, Mary?"

"Lifestyle of impatience — I've got no time for it."

"Mary, go ahead and dump me by the curb, but don't think that your life is suddenly going to be instantly different. The problem, Mary, is you. It's not me. Amputating me won't be the quick fix you think."

"It'll be a nice start."

"Thanks."

"No, thank YOU, Dave. It's nice that you're finally looking me in the eye and talking to me. Don't forget for the past twenty-five years I've been a work widow, a sports widow, and lately, an Internet widow. Dave, we've been divorced for a long time; you just never bothered to notice because the services weren't discontinued."

"Darling, 'service' isn't exactly what I'd call last night. You've been phoning it in for a dog's age."

* * *

In time, divorce can be a good thing. It can allow people to start again. A new perspective can be gained. Mary may travel the world, make love to a stranger on the beach, and sell her creations to world fame — or she may wonder what she and Dave could have done years ago to make their marriage work.

Would it have been worth the effort?

Dave may lease a twin turbo, date a couple of hot women with screaming kids, spend a few grand on space-age golf clubs and — and he may wonder, everyday perhaps, what he could have done to better support Mary's aspirations.

When people feel a lump on their body, they see a doctor as soon as possible. When people sleep next to one, they'll wait five, ten, maybe twenty-five years to do something.

When I come to bed, often late at night, sometimes I listen to my wife breathing, and I think to myself how impossibly lucky I am that she stays with me, puts up with me, appears to listen to my utterly stupid thoughts, and then, as I lay my head on the pillow, I wonder if I am really the partner she needs me to be. Together, we should be better than we are individually. Or am I just a lump?

How about you? Does your marriage need some attention? Is your marriage what it could be? Marriage should make us stronger, more inspired, more caring. How many years will you wait?

Love is a Decision

*"Love is patient, love is kind. It does not envy, it does not boast,
it is not proud. It is not rude, it is not self-seeking, it is not easily
angered, it keeps no record of wrongs."*
— CORINTHIANS

Who has not pulled the petals from a daisy? She loves you. She loves you not. You repeat the words, hoping. Wondering.

You love me. You love me not.

When you are young, love comes likes a storm into your heart. Love can overtake you, sweep you up. Love can destroy your sense of balance. Love can take you for a roller coaster ride.

When you are older, love becomes a thief in the night. It is there. It is not there. Your parents tell you to work at it, but you find yourself slipping away. Why should love be like hard work?

Why can't love be easy?

The love in youth and the love of experience are two different things. Yet in youth, we mistake our infatuations for mature devotion. We want to grow up too fast; we want to join the adult community who, we do not realize, struggle everyday with love.

With experience, we realize that our childhood notions of love will continue unless they are replaced by a more mature love, a deeper love, a love that is more akin to faith than emotion.

Those of us who have been divorced or think of separation know that romantic love holds little promise for those who do not love themselves. Self love, then, becomes the basis by which others recognize and are attracted by our bouquet of strengths.

What is self love? Is it bragging? Is it self-aggrandizing? Does it mean you stand in front of mirrors a lot?

Self love means agency. It means power, the freedom to choose. It means that you delight in your personal strengths. It means you respect yourself, take care of yourself, and forgive yourself.

Compassion comes from the kind of self love that declares itself open, vulnerable, and resilient.

I would walk a thousand miles for you. To have true agency requires a sense of self-security. People with a sense of self-security are capable of a resilience that enables them to overcome difficulty, find jobs in foreign places, bounce back from tragedy.

Those without this level of security often lead quiet yet desperate lives. I feel trapped. I feel stuck. The choices are few; the path narrow; the doubts many.

I am lost, you say. I am not worthy of love, you say. Nothing comes easy, you say.

I am nothing, you say finally.

From the bottom of despair, from the heart of darkness, there is something that teaches you a universal truth. From the lowest of the lows, the most reckless of the reckless, there is something that teaches you a universal truth.

What truth? What wisdom?

That you are great. Yes, you are. That you are deserving of the greatest of love. That good things will come your way and surround you. That in nothingness is found this small little secret: you create your own experiences.

If you are tormented by your desires, you can calm your heart and desire nothing but what you already have.

If you are tormented by sadness, you can release your anger, forgive yourself, and see sadness for what it is, an emotion, a mechanism, a direction that can be changed by movement – the quick effort of a telephone call, the transformation of a simple walk in the February rain, a long embrace.

We cannot make up in one February day for all our difficulties and challenges, but we can begin the day with an exhortation: I am worthy of love. I deserve deep and meaningful love. I am found. When

I was young, I looked up into the clouds and wondered how my life would be. I would lie down on the cool grass and look up into the blue sky and wonder. If I closed my eyes tight, I thought I could feel the earth turning beneath my body. Where am I going? Who will I be? Who will love me?

Today, I am defined not by my net worth, my occupation, my possessions, but by those who love me.

Those who love you. My wife, my children, my family and friends. Those who love you. Your ancestors, your great, great family. Who loves you?

And all of us here wish you great love, the kind of love that begins in a private yet vast relationship between you and the universe, the love that whispers in your ear at the worst of times – yes, you are worthy of great love.

Give and it shall be yours, say the paradoxical words of our knowledge bearers. Let go of desire and your heart will be full, the wisest of the wise tell us.

The petals of the daisy float on the wind. You love me. You love me not. Me. Or not me.

To be or not to be, that is the question, exhorts the great dramatist.

And to be, to really *be*, is a courageous decision about recognizing the fullness of this singular moment. Stand up and be loved. Say the words out aloud: I am worthy of great love.

You are worthy.

But how do you love? How do you love?

With reckless joy. With an open heart. With an abundant faith. Like a single petal floating on the wind. You are never alone.

Father, Soldier, Revolutionary, Spy – Part I

At first she did nothing because that was her nature. My mother felt his hands upon her throat. He was yelling something at her. She could smell his stale breath. His eyes were narrowed and his jaw firm. Madness erupted in his eyes.

She had been dreaming.

He shook her, and she struggled for air. She thought about death. She considered closing her eyes and allowing him murder.

Why not give him his way?

He was her husband. She followed him dutifully. He had been the biggest influence in her life. They had been married in a small church in 1961, surrounded by security forces. They went to the sandy beaches of Pusan for their honeymoon, swimming on the beach, posing on a rock for a photograph, making love again and again in their hotel room. She has given him two children, followed him to Canada, worked as a campus chambermaid, and lived dutifully as a minister's wife.

She twisted sideways. The room darkened. She looked through the venetian blinds and glimpsed a corner of the blue sky. Fading, fading.

This is not my husband, she told herself and twisted her body sideways. This is mental illness. She gasped for air and rolled her knees upward. She thrust outward and pushed him backward. He fell off the bed. He banged his head against a bookshelf.

She dashed out of the room. She ran out of the apartment, coughing and crying. Her throat began to swell.

My mother met my father in Korea during the sixties when she came to military intelligence as a French translator.

It wasn't long before she entered a training program. They asked what kind of career she dreamed about. She told them broadcaster. And so they groomed her, trained her, and prepared her for a position in broadcasting. Few assets were more valuable than those who worked in the media.

That was what he told her before he decided to keep her as his own.

No doubt she found his power and influence attractive. He was a charismatic, intense young man with a burning intellect and a disarming smile.

They shared some common values. He had been raised on Cheju under Japanese occupation. She had been raised under Japanese occupation in Manchuria. Among other things, they both enjoyed Japanese food. She loved fashion, dancing, dogs, and jewelry. He loved fishing, reading, swimming, and politics. When he went abroad, he brought back Chanel perfume. Throughout my childhood, I remember most the times my mother packed her bags and told us she had to get away. At five years old, I remember telling her not to leave us with him. At ten, I insisted she get a divorce. At fifteen, I practiced karate so that I would be ready to help her escape.

When I was a boy, I did not know the things that I know now. How could I know what kind of father I had? How could I know what he whispered to my mother to keep her from leaving.

I was her son. I grew up knowing that there were things she wanted that my father could not give. But, aside from small things, I didn't know what she needed. She often told us how things would have been different if she had had a career as a journalist.

"Then, you would have married another man, and we wouldn't exist," I would say.

"I know," she would sigh. "I know."

They were my parents. I knew only them. I had no other comparisons. I did not know what kind of family I belonged to. I did not know what was normal. The pictures on our black and white television of families like the Bunkers, the Waltons, the Bradys only made me wonder more.

In retrospect, I realize that all children feel this way. Our families are strange and wonderful. The people who feed us, raise us, and transfer their values to us are also connected to the past and to their own families.

Our ancestors become us.

The line that connects us goes spiraling backward and we realize that connection cannot be broken, no matter how we try, no matter what we become.

So, when I put my father into a mental institution, removed my mother from her home and moved her across town, I wondered if they had somehow prepared me to be my parents' caregiver, for I never failed to live up to my duties as the first son.

I did my duty. I heeded my father's word. He told me to take care of him if he ever got violent. I heeded my responsibility to my mother. We got her government job back through political contacts and old friends. We found her an apartment in Kitsilano near the beach. But the one thing I could not do was go to the Burnaby Psychiatric Centre and see my father.

In truth, I was afraid.

Even though I was a grown man, thirty-two years old, an English professor with a family of my own, I became a helpless child in the company of my father who was five foot five and 130 pounds. It was more than just the schizophrenia.

My love for him had manifested itself in two ways: firstly, in acts of mutiny and revolt; secondly, in desperate acts of a son seeking his father's approval.

I have spent a good deal of my life reaching out to my father. I desperately wanted his endorsement, his admiration. He is connected to me in ways that I do not understand. He is my sail and my anchor, my father and my tormentor, my inspiration and my foe. He had been a deadly soldier, a political revolutionary, and a charismatic preacher.

But to me, he was my dad.

As I thought these things one blustery day in 1992, the telephone rang.

It was a male nurse from the psychiatric ward. My father had demanded to know who was responsible for his incarceration. The nurses were shocked by his command, his vocabulary, and his forcefulness. When one of the nurses tried to give him a sedative, my father moved decisively. He quickly overwhelmed three male nurses, breaking a nose, and removing an elbow from its proper position, and escaped.

The RCMP had been notified. They asked me where he might go. I told them that I didn't know.

I knew he was coming for me.

Father, Soldier, Revolutionary, Spy – Part II

In August of 1992, two RCMP officers came to the door of my parents' condo and told me the news: my father had escaped. He had overpowered three male nurses and somehow slipped out of the locked mental facility in Burnaby. One of the nurses had a dislocated arm, the other a busted nose. "Does your father have martial arts training?" the tall officer asked.

"A black belt," I mumbled. My father taught karate every Thursday night when I was a teenager in Williams Lake.

"It says here that he's a retired minister."

"Yup," I said. I didn't tell them that in addition to commando training, he ran the Korean CIA in the early sixties, a force with thousands of employees, including the French translator he would marry, my mother. I also left out the part about him wearing a concealed handgun in Seoul and sleeping with it under the pillow.

"Do you have any idea where your father might be? He's got no money or identification."

"And, he's got no shoes," said the tall officer.

"I don't know where he could be," I said, looking out at the Coast Mountains. The afternoon sky was like concrete. I felt a sick feeling coming over me. I was thirty-two years old. My father was a slender, shy, senior who weighed maybe 130 pounds.

And I was still afraid of him.

* * *

A few months before my father's big escape, he and my mother visited me in Prince George where I taught college English.

It was the last weekend in May, a brief moment that we northerners call spring. The apple tree in my front yard sported little white flowers. They parked their '86 Toyota van out in front. The Mercedes had been long sold. "Why are you sleeping in the van, Dad? I've got a perfectly acceptable bed you can use. I'll sleep in the basement. It's no trouble."

"I prefer it for safety reasons," he said.

"Is that why you're lining your fishing hat with tin foil?" I said.

"Don't you question me!" he shouted and walked out.

***

Mental illness is fairly challenging for any family, to put it mildly. If you listen to the doctors, you learn to separate the illness from the person.

It was the illness that caused my father to try to choke the life out of my mother. It was the illness that made him believe he could pick lottery numbers, thereby forcing my mother to quit her government job. It was the illness that caused him to point out the invisible creatures that were sitting on people's shoulders.

"Want me to drown the little 'flabby devil' on your shoulder?"

"What's the little guy doing?"

"He's staring at his friends around your feet."

What made my father's illness particularly problematic was the fifty-fifty principle: half of what my dad said was utterly ridiculous. For example, he worried that Mom was poisoning his food. He worried that North Korean soldiers were invading the condo.

I thought I was cool with the crazy stuff. But what really got me was the other fifty percent – the "half-true" stuff.

He suggested to my sister that a certain old family friend was a pedophile. My sister, when she heard this, refused to talk about it – other than saying that yes, this was probably true. I think it was true. My father was obsessed with sexuality, religion, and literary figures. He talked about people's auras. He talked about the spirit world. He spoke to the dead. He talked as if he was tapped into the timeless unseen world in a way that made my skin crawl. At times, I desperately wanted to talk to someone, but nobody wants to talk about mental illness.

On his visit, I couldn't stand the half-truths anymore, so I called the local paranormal society.

"My father says he sees ghosts and spirits. You wouldn't happen to know any people who can verify this kind of stuff?"

"Sure, we'll be right over." I imagined the van from the film the Ghostbusters pulling up to the house, but instead a man and two women arrived together in a rather tired Ford Tempo. If you had access to unseen power and vision, wouldn't you make a better choice of automobile?

They said hello to my father who I dragged out of the Toyota, so I could put him on display. One of the women acted like a medium because she closed her eyes a lot and fingered the white crystals around her neck. The younger of the women had long black hair with a tie-dyed bandana around it. The man wore a trimmed beard, wire-framed glasses, and carried himself as if he were the leader. Actually, he looked more like a guy who might be good at fixing computers.

My father answered a few questions and said, "I'm going to leave now. Please accept your homosexuality, sir. And I can smell the illness in you women. Go see a doctor. You have internal problems." The three sat silently and listened to the front door slam.

"Your father's aura is black," said the woman with the tie-dyed bandana.

"What does that mean?" I said. The man spoke slowly, rubbing his eyes.

"It means that he's very difficult to read. Your father's very troubled. I'm not getting a good feeling."

"And his power is rather ... daunting."

"Really," I said. "What should I do?"

"There is nothing we can do to help. Just think about the white light."

"What about his self-hypnosis?" I said. "What about his conversations with General Douglas MacArthur? What about all that stuff he said about your homosexuality, sir?"

"Fill yourself with white light. We have to leave," said the man. So that was that. My father scared off the paranormals. Everybody was scared. I was scared. My mother was scared. My doctor's family was scared. The cops were scared.

* * *

I rented a science fiction movie and asked my friend Wing Sui to come over. I told him I was scared. You don't talk like that, he said, and came over. I told him in self-pity, my father is on the loose and he holds me responsible.

At around 8 p.m., there was a knock on the door. I looked in the peephole with my heart racing. It was the police officers, Laurel and Hardy. My father had been spotted. He had spent the day on the eighth floor, visiting with some retired folks. He was gone again, this time with shoes and money. He had been in the building the whole time.

Later that night, I tried to close my eyes. I could hear the jumbled, chaotic sounds of the city. I could not sleep. I was waiting to hear him calling my name from below, my Korean name, the name he used when I was a boy.

When I came to Canada, I cried at night a lot. He always sat on the edge of my bed, touching my forehead.

I heard sirens. The traffic lights reflected on the ceiling. It was hot, so I opened the windows and blinds. Someone in the condo above watched a religious channel. A man was preaching.

In Prince George, those few nights my parents visited, I could not sleep either. I slept downstairs. For the first time in my life, I faced a kind of fear that I can only call supernatural. My mind was jagged in ways I cannot describe. Before I rented the house, someone killed himself in it. In the darkness, I thought I heard voices, and felt myself on the verge of disappearing. What must it have been like to lose your mind? Oh, the fear.

I could not stop my fear until I filled myself with a simple realization: it was the disease talking, not him. It was the disease talking, not my father. It was my guilt, fear and sorrow talking, not my own version of his disease.

The next day I saw him.

Father, Soldier, Revolutionary, Spy – Part III

Hi, Dad, I said. He was stretched out on a narrow cot. He opened his eyes and stared up at the ceiling without blinking. My father wore a faded golf shirt, khakis, and jogging shoes. His hands were folded over his chest as if he were in a coffin.

The lights were off. A narrow window provided a faint glow. The traffic sounds were muted. A woman wearing headphones operated a gas-powered trimmer along the edge of the building. Rat, tat, tat, tat.

Go right in, said the nurse, a tall man with a clipboard and a beard. You dad's been getting some shut-eye. He had a hint of tattoo, barbed wire peaking out of his short-sleeved shirt.

The nurse smiled and moved a chair. A few minutes earlier we had chatted about my father's background.

Yeah, man, he had said. Your old man's like a priest-slash-warrior, a soldier, founding father of Korea, a United Church minister.

Yeah, he set the bar, I had said.

The psychiatric centre on Willingdon Avenue in Burnaby had two sets of locked doors. There was plenty of visitor parking even though there were at least thirty beds. You could see why nobody wanted to visit the place. The wind had pushed a pile of orange leaves against the single door entrance. The place looked abandoned.

I wanted to skulk away and go back to my hotel. Instead, I grabbed the door and opened it.

In the 1990's the BC government closed a place called Riverview Hospital in Coquitlam. It was an infamous institution, a place where you put people away. Apparently, they let a lot of people on the street when they closed — to be "reabsorbed" by their communities.

Now, I imagined, everyone was on the loose, under overpasses, in rooming houses, on couches, and in emergency rooms. When the police found my father, they handcuffed him and took him to Burnaby General where he sat in a rubber room without any furniture for twelve hours. They thought he would harm himself.

How did this all happen?

I looked at my father. His eyes looked empty. He was thoroughly medicated. He blinked slowly like he was slowing down time. I sat down on the chair beside the bed.

Who are you? he asked.

I'm just checking up on you.

I don't know who you are.

I'm your son. You have a son and daughter. Stan and Heidi. You named us. We are your family.

Get out. You're not my family.

Hey. I am your son, I said. He looked away. I watched him blink. Dad, I put you here.

What?

I put you here.

You? Why?

Because you told me to. Because you said that it was my job to look after you and Mom. Because I'm your son.

You are nothing. My father's shoulders slumped.

Okay, I said. I am nothing. His eyes softened. I moved to the bed and put my hand on his shoulder. His shoulders were bony. The rat-tat-tat from the trimmer stopped.

He began to sob then, shoulders shaking, nose running.

Are you okay, Dad?

Why did you say I wasn't a good daddy? he asked, recalling a telephone conversion I had had with him a few months before. After his spring visit to Prince George, he called and wanted to know why I had not visited him more.

Why? he had asked. So I told him in words I had never used before.

I said, Because. Because you were not a good father to me. It was the voice of the child, his child, the one who was still angry. He hung up right away. I phoned back. He sobbed and then he hung up again.

And now, in the middle of a psychiatric holding cell, my father wanted to know if I really meant what I had said – you were not a good father to me.

Why did you say that? he asked. I looked at my father. The skin around his eyelids sagged. I thought of how many Sundays I stood at the front of the church after the service was over, waiting, like all the others to shake his hand. How he would look right through me and then past me to the others.

Dad, I said carefully. I have been a bad son. You have been a good father. You made me strong. You listen to me now, okay? You listen to me. Tears flowed from my eyes and I choked out some more words. I am sorry. I didn't take care of you properly. I should have.

* * *

On my father's neck there was a scar, a small white line. I once asked my father on one of those terrible nights when I used to cry where he got the scar.

How did you get it, Daddy?

It's from a bullet. Now go to sleep.

From a gun?

Yes, he said. You used to play with my combat helmet when you were small. The helmet had many marks from bullets.

What did you want to be when you were a boy, Dad? When you were eight years old?

I wanted to be president of my country, he said. I lived under Japanese occupation on Cheju Island. I dreamed of an independent Korea.

Daddy?

Yes, son?

What will I be? What will I be? Will I fight in wars? Will I start a coup?

You, my son, you will be a man of principle.

I will.

Whenever I recall that conversation, I feel my father to be larger than life, a man of great wisdom and purpose. A man who began a country, ministered to hundreds, and raised two children. He was the man I had wanted so much to impress. He was the man I would ultimately disappoint.

* * *

When I was thirty years old, my father became very ill. He hurt my mother, and I had to take action. I signed the paperwork and made sure he received treatment, even though it was against his will, even though I would lose him.

I have accepted my role in his life.

I tried to take care of him, but I couldn't. I was not able to overcome my feelings. For the next decade, my sister who is generous and dispassionate took care of his affairs. I listened to my sister who would tell me how much the social workers and nurses enjoyed him.

I have not met any of these people.

And then on a fall morning a few years ago, my father announced to the hospice nursing staff that it was a good day to die.

I think he had been waiting a long time to be able to say something like that.

He is reported to have spoken the words with energy and precision, even though his stomach cancer was causing him great pain. Of course, he refused pain killers, preferring to meditate.

Then my father walked to his room at the end of the hall, put away his meagre belongings, took off his shoes, folded his hands across his chest, and closed his eyes.

First Cast – Part I

East of Horsefly the road begins to get steeper and the surface becomes harder; the deep potholes have a way of destroying suspension and breaking axles. My father kept a steady pace, floating the truck over the loose gravel on the shoulders, and slowing down on the rough spots so that the bolts on the boat trailer didn't shake loose.

Even the spruce blackened and sharpened as we ascended. Lichen-covered and too narrow for saw mills, the spruce seemed foreign, more triangular, less like trees, more like wild and uncaring spires. The mountain lake my father and I were headed to was deep in classic moose and blackfly country. Few people lived this far into the bush. Everything human-made that we passed, whether it was a sign, a fence, or a barn, seemed bleached by the mountain air and overgrown with fireweed and paintbrush.

Everything built by human hands was quickly consumed and made unfamiliar. Three-quarters of the way there, my father wanted a pit stop, so we pulled the truck over at a small resort on Morrison Lake. I stepped out and stretched. The air smelled clean and the insides of my nostrils felt raw. The sun was a bright halo, and it felt hot on your arms, but you could feel the chill in the wind when it rose off the lake. In the bluish hazy east, you could see faded mountains.

I put together my spinning rod and headed out to a small, skinny dock for a few casual casts. I don't know why my father loves fishing so much. Maybe he fished a lot as a boy. Maybe it meant escaping the business of the United Church for a while. Lately, he had been doing a lot of marriage counseling which he found extremely taxing. I found ironic most of the things he was known for in the community. We did not see him that way.

I had thought the same thing when, on his first post, he started a teen youth group in Maryfield, Saskatchewan, where the teens danced and listened to Blind Faith and Leonard Cohen. When he became popular with the teenagers, my sister and I shook our heads. Maybe it was something deeper than the church that brought him out to the wilderness. Maybe it was how he felt out at a remote mountain lake, all alone, except for his quiet twelve-year-old son. Perhaps it was some quasi-romantic connection he had with nature. Maybe this was his church. Maybe he just liked eating trout. I never knew if it was escape or contentment or recreation. And I never really knew what I was doing there.

The water was clear and deep around the dock, so I tied on a small spoon with three red spots on it that was heavy enough to cast into the afternoon breeze. I knew that this particular lure was also heavy enough to sink to where the big fish waited. On the first cast, I felt something grab the lure. The line pulled heavily a second time, and I set the hook with my wrists, pulling up on my rod tip. I looked around to see if my father was around. I felt my heart beating outside my chest. First cast, I thought to myself. I felt alive, even if nobody was around to see me. First cast!

The trout took the lure and went for a long run, pulling away twenty yards of six-pound line. I adjusted the drag on the spinning reel and when the trout was done pulling, I began to slowly guide him back to me. I was thrilled but calm, and things felt as they should feel to a twelve-year-old boy, real and weighty and actual. I squinted and covered my eyes to look for places where the fish might get hung up. On my left there was a stump sticking out of the water, so I walked out to the end of the dock while slowly reeling in. I noticed a pair of wood ducks sailing quietly along the edge of the reedy shoreline. I felt the air leaving my lungs. The dark blue on the male duck's wing matched a point on the horizon toward the mountains.

The trout felt very heavy, but I reeled in quickly because I wanted to land the fish and be lounging in the truck before my dad realized I did anything. I wanted to be the Great Fisherman, the guy who could catch a fish while the others were taking a piss. It would be so great. Without a net, I know I had to be very careful. Trout get crazy active as soon as they see it's you. I squatted down on one knee as I pulled the fish in. I didn't want the trout to see me. I'd have him on the dock, and then I'd have him gutted in thirty seconds flat, and then I'd jump into the truck with the fish wrapped in newspaper when my father returned from the can.

I'd present it to him as a gift, a gift to my father. This is how I thought as I kid. These are the kinds of things I thought I needed to do to impress my father.

Beneath the water, I saw the trout, spotted, green and twisting. For a brief moment, I saw its rainbow-coloured sides catch the light. I saw that it was hooked lightly on its lower lip. I heard my father coming toward me from behind. I didn't look at him. I spoke matter-of-factly, trying to stay calm. Get the net, I said. I tell you. She's big. Then I felt my dad jump off the dock and heard him run back to the truck with change shaking his pockets.

I looked down into the water. The trout was probably about six pounds, at least three times bigger than what I usually caught. It was certainly bigger than anything my father had ever caught. I kept my rod tip up. I kept tension on the line. I could hear the truck door open and close, and I could hear him running back toward me, but I was running out of time. I contemplated reaching down and grabbing the trout's head and lifting him out, but that was an extremely risky move. The fish wanted to take another run, and I didn't know what to do. If I let the fish run again, he could get some slack in the line, shake the hook, and get free. If I held him tight, he could easily snap the line. It was only six-pound line.

When my father reached the dock, I yelled out, don't bounce on the dock! And so he walked slowly toward me with the aluminum net in his hand. I could hear him breathing heavily.

Is he still on? Yup, I said. Pass me the net. And stay low. I'll get him for you, he said firmly. I could feel his shadow on top of me. Its coolness felt like a distant cloud. I could feel his weight pushing down on the dock. I felt his shadow moving out over the water. And I felt the fish snap the line. Suddenly, my hands felt dead of weight, empty and utterly free of tension.

It's gone, I said quietly. I was angry and disappointed and hateful. That was my best lure. You spooked him. How big was it? he asked. It was the biggest trout in the goddamn world. Well, you lost it, he said. That's too bad. I followed him back to the truck. I put away the rod and the net and got back into the truck. My father's apology policy remained straightforward: he only said sorry if he beat me. But it never took long for us to be afraid again.

Otherwise, he would never say sorry. Ever.

First Cast – Part II

When we were back on the road again, I thought about how anxious my father was every time he had a fish on the line. His eyes would go all buggy, and he'd have extreme panic in his voice. He was so nervous when he had a fish on that if my mother was around, he'd blame her for anything that went wrong. The more I fished, the better I got, and the more praise my mother would heap on me, especially when I started out-fishing my father.

A word of advice to twelve-year-old boys: out-fishing your dad is not a great thing to do. When we arrived at the lake, we weren't quite sure if we were at the right lake. The lake was unmarked, and if there was a sign, it had probably been erased by the forces of nature. I had read somewhere that this lake was carved out of glacial movement. It was very, very deep lake. I suppose that's why we chose it as our destination. We thought the fish would be big. We found a place to park near a stand of birch. Although it was the middle of summer, the leaves had already begun to fade.

I set up the inside of the camper for sleeping while my father unhitched the trailer and went looking for firewood. The sun had disappeared and the sky was violet. A pair of loons sailed in the distance, and the air was still and cool. I killed all the mosquitoes in the camper, got dressed for bed, turned off the light, and lay on top of my sleeping bag.

I wondered if I would dream about that massive, six-pound, primordial trout. An hour or so later, my father walked toward the camper. I heard him brushing his teeth outside. He entered the camper and took off his clothes. I could smell the campfire on his clothing. I opened my eyes and watched for a moment. He had a broad smile on his face. I had shaped my anger into a tight ball. I had not spoken a word to my father since the fish incident nine hours before. Now he was smiling.

I didn't say good night. I didn't comment upon the drive. We hadn't said a word, but my silence had had no effect. I rolled over and closed my angry eyes. An apology would have been a simple thing, but it is I who am sorry now, sorry that I turned everything inward into silence. But truly, that was my only option, and I learned it all from him. That's the kind of son I was.

The next morning, we woke early. I looked down at my legs and they were covered with blood. Tiny no-seeums, small enough to enter through the screens, had chewed on my legs all night. I wiped the blood away and joined my father outside. I didn't need to feel, I reasoned.

Everything was wrapped in mist. We stood eating Fig Newtons. It was wet and cool, but I was anxious. The earlier we got our lines wet, the better our results. I heard a loon call in the distance. We did not speak until we had pushed our aluminum boat into the water. My father put the motor in the water and began priming it with fuel.

Dad, why don't we drift out a ways and I'll row? He grunted, and I grabbed the oars. I could tell he was irritated about moving from trolling to casting, but he quickly unsnapped the gang troll and snapped on a spoon. My father used snap-on leads, whereas I always tied my lures on. I was serious about fishing.

My father stood up and started casting while I sharpened the hooks on my spinning lure. My father never sharpened his hooks. The air was crisp and the fog made us feel even more isolated and more alone. We could barely see where we had made camp. The truck disappeared into the distance. There was no wind at all. It was eerie how still and calm everything felt. It was like everything was dead. I can sense fish, I said. This made my father smile. He put a worm onto his hook. He passed the worm can to me. I put the worm can down. You're not going to use a worm? he asked.

Nope. Why not? I don't need live bait. We cast out and heard our lures plop into the water. I turned off the ticking on my reel so that we could be extra quiet. In an hour or so, it would be light.

Fish, my dad said quietly as he brought in a splashing rainbow trout. It was at least fifteen inches long, a sleek two-and-a-half pounder. I grabbed the net and brought it into the boat.

My father put a new worm on his hook, threading the hook through its fat body several times. He dipped his wormy fingers into the water and then he cast out again. The fish flopped around, threatening to jump out of the boat. It was a noisy trout with its gills vibrating and its tail flapping. The fish bounced from the front of the boat where I sat to the back of the boat.

We had forgotten to bring something to kill the fish with, so I grabbed the fish and put my thumb into its rough mouth. I pressed backward and snapped the neck. I put my hands overboard and washed the blood into the water. I had never killed like this before, and I felt powerful for a moment, as if I could live forever. You can feel pretty strong when you're trying not to feel.

I stood up and cast out my lure and retrieved it slowly. Usually when I fished, I would concentrate with all my might on the action of the lure and of the connection between the water and me. But this time, I decided to let my mind wander. I wanted to luxuriate in the dawn. I wanted to remember this moment on the lake.

He was smiling again. Beaming like this was perfection. This? We were ghosts fishing on a grey morning in the middle of nowhere. Suddenly I didn't care about fishing anymore. I let my hand trail in the water when my father turned on the motor and started to troll. Let my father catch all the fish, I said to myself. Let him smile. Let me be his son. Let him be my father in the way that he knows. I closed my eyes trying to feel the warm of the morning on my face, but the fog would not burn off until noon.

Electric Fear

Airports are fascinating points of intersection. They are an interstitial place, a borderland where one world meets another, where ideas, emotions, and values collide. Despite our frantic and heightened attention to All-Mighty security, airports are usually where people kiss, embrace, and scurry back to their homes.

Airports are not places where people die.

Today, in countries everywhere, the airport symbolizes a space where we have crossed the line from humanity to inhumanity. The airport is a site of pain that represents who we are at our worst, a species moved by the least noble of sentiments.

The fingers point everywhere in the tragic death of Robert Dziekanski, our disoriented Polish visitor. We watch him flail, convulse, and die, accompanied by the unnatural soundtrack of 50,000 volts of electricity. What can we learn from this horrific event? What does this tragic event say about us?

Some prefer to point their fingers at the obvious, the de-evolution of our once mighty RCMP, today a fallen institution searching for a new identity. We wonder what has happened to our once proud symbol of restraint and fairness.

Our noble officers, our dedicated sons and daughters, are not without responsibility, and some are making spirited calls for criminal charges. I have to ask, were these individuals provided the appropriate education and training to deal with our ever-increasing and complex threats?

Some say that the RCMP is the easy target, the media fall guy. The RCMP may have it coming, but another culprit is the taser itself, a bloodless weapon touted to save lives and fatten pockets. In my view, the taser is no more to blame than electricity.

Those in other countries watching the scene on CNN suggest a possible contributor, the growing intolerance in Canada, once a nation of peace-keeping immigrants, now a fumbling bunch of A-Team wannabes who can't summon an interpreter in order to calm a tired and unarmed visitor, or perform life-saving action after repeated taser strikes.

How do you feel when you watch other, less-free countries put our country on their travel advisories? I cannot help but shake my head and wonder: Oh, Canada, Canada, Canada. This is the true north strong and free – how could it be dangerous to visit? What has become of us?

If we blame anything or anyone, it should not be the RCMP, the makers of Taser, frazzled airport workers, or those who still believe we have become too much like our neighbours. No, most who have experience in crisis situations know the real culprit.

Fear.

When fear strikes hold, you are capable of imagining and seeing the worst. When fear strikes hold, you lose your confidence in your own humanity. Ask any police officer, social worker, gated home developer, teacher, or terrorist: nothing is more powerful than fear.

Fear will make you drown your best friend. Fear will make you shoot your toddler at midnight. Fear alone summons our greatest demons. In times of national crisis, fear makes us turn on each other. Ask all those citizens who have been interned or forced onto reserves.

It makes us less than human.

Fear compels us to behave in ways that destroy our ideals. It makes us wary of toothpaste and hair gel. It makes us consider umbrellas as life-threatening. I take off my shoes at the airport and wonder which is a bigger threat – crepe soles or cotton shoelaces.

Fear makes us justify despicable, laughable, and unnecessary acts.

When fear struck the airport personnel, who could blame them for calling the police? When fear struck the police, who could blame them for trying out their shiny new weapons? Who can blame the officer who kneeled on a dying man's neck?

The airport is the post-modern locus of our greatest nightmares: terrorism, hijackers, hostages, and unimaginatively bad shopping. It all unravels like a tensor bandage gone awry as you and I (and the guy over there who can't speak English) become threats — depersonalized and treated with unspeakable indifference.

A crack-head will kick open a door tonight. Somewhere else in our native land a child will be abducted. At your local school, someone will threaten someone. A man will be beaten outside a bar for no reason. On Sunday morning, if you are walking in any downtown, you will see fresh blood on the sidewalk. And at Canadian airports forevermore, we'll hug each other, but never feel quite safe.

We frail, frightened and highly-armed human beings have every reason to be afraid. Look at what we are capable of in a hockey game or in a marriage. Wives are afraid of their husbands and vice-versa. Neighbours make neighbours nervous. Teachers are afraid of their students. What is the result of all this palpable emotion? What is the terrorist's true objective? What is the bully's true objective? What is the enforcer's true objective?

Fear makes cowards of us all.

Nothing can change a community or a country or a family as quickly as fear. And so, we ask, what is the antidote? What can we do to make sure that a minor everyday conflict does not end in cruel death?

Is the answer more high tech weaponry, video cameras, strip searches, and confiscated hair mousse?

Listen. So much depends upon our ears. Our eyes betray us. When our hearts are racing, our eyes do not see straight. But our ears, if we use them, can tell us the truth and the truth is very basic: we are all lost children.

All we want to do is go home.

Conflict resolution is just a fancy term for the simplest of acts, the act of listening. "What language do you speak? How are you?

Are you okay? What can I do to make you feel more comfortable? I know you are afraid. So am I. Let's work this out together."

Robert Dziekanski was 40. He died on October 14, ten hours after he landed at Vancouver International Airport. He was on his way to Kamloops to live with his mother.

The Power of Self-Forgiveness

"Without forgiveness, there's no future." — DESMOND TUTU
"Forgiveness is the fragrance that the violet sheds on the heel that has crushed it." — MARK TWAIN

I could write a list of goals for every aspect of my life. I could eat better, get more exercise, spend more prudently, be kinder, and find more compassion. Easy, eh?

Okay, not really.

This last category of compassion intrigues me a great deal because compassion is much more challenging than it appears. I have sat in churches looking for it. I have even given talks on the subject. I have donated my time and energy to non-profit organizations. Heck, I think I even cry at all the right times in movies, but I don't feel that I am yet a compassionate person.

If I cannot find more compassion in my life, then I wonder if I can make a difference. We all keep up with the news and try not to absorb its full import, but let's state the obvious: the world is in deep trouble, not just economically, not just environmentally, but psychologically.

In the words written here, I have expressed a kind of stress or pain that crosses the boundaries of generations and time. My father and mother were joyous and deeply troubled people. My grandmother allowed bitterness and anger to crush her hopes. The country of my origin, Korea, has suffered greatly under decades of occupation.

I know this sounds odd, but I feel this strange, generational pain as a numbness, an angst, a sadness, not about our potential as human beings to achieve our goals, but our inability to confront the biggest obstacle of all: our inability to forgive ourselves.

If we cannot forgive ourselves, then compassion becomes impossible. Try on this thought if you can: if we can forgive ourselves, then the world can change, then we can collectively break the cycle of pain that locks us into generations of war, violence, and vengeance.

Forgiveness makes compassion possible; with compassion will come a new life on this planet.

At ground zero in New York, a priest wants to build a garden of compassion like the one under construction in Beirut. A good idea for some, a terrible idea for others. We all know that forgiveness heals, but that doesn't mean it can be forced.

A friend is writing an important study about the life cycle of monuments. She describes how and why we build monuments, how they represent a community's highest ideals, and how they evolve over time.

She describes how a monument like the one built to commemorate the sacrifices of the Vietnam War helped America forgive its soldiers and itself. This work, as you can imagine, is extremely taxing because it makes you think about yourself, your influences, your world, your pain.

I still remember the sunrise ceremony hosted by the Metepenagiag people of the Mi'kmaq First Nation. We sat on the banks of the Miramichi in New Brunswick. On June 11, 2008, our prime minister apologized for the wrongs committed in residential schools:

"The treatment of children in Indian residential schools is a sad chapter in our history. Today, we recognize that this policy of assimilation was wrong, has caused great harm, and has no place in our country."

Two aboriginal women at our sunrise ceremony sobbed. I feel that this day was an important step in healing for not just aboriginal people, but this nation. When I think of compassion I think of falling into the arms of these women. They held me, just as much as I held them.

In my own journey, I must start with the things that I cannot forgive about myself. When I harm others, when I exclude, when I disrespect difference, when I do not keep my word – when I do these things I damage others. I dishonour my ancestors, my planet, and myself.

If I cannot forgive myself, if I cannot move beyond the obstacles in my heart, I will always be intolerant of others and myself. This is what I must NOT do: continue the cycle of pain and suffering. In the space between living and dreaming, my ancestors expect me to break this cycle.

My mentors tell me that to grow as a human being, to appreciate all that life has to offer, is not about reaching the pinnacle of material, intellectual, or physical success. Life is not about winning, scoring the biggest toys, or looking down from the top. Life is about love, my mentors say, but sometimes, I just don't get it.

Love is the subject of every pop song, countless clichés, and every other trinket in your favourite store, but that does not mean that love is accessible. I want to open my heart, but where is the door?

How does one forgive oneself? When my children ask me how to get good at anything, I always respond with the same exhortation: practice.

So I guess I will practice self-forgiveness.

I forgive myself for not taking better care of my dying mother. I forgive myself for giving her cancer, even though I know this is impossible. I forgive myself for being unable to help my father, so lost was I in anger and denial and immaturity. I forgive myself for being so selfish, so focused on the wrong things, so average. I forgive myself for not exceeding expectations, for squandering my insights, for not loving myself and others fully, for holding onto anger and resentment. I forgive myself for being vengeful.

I don't know if I have the courage to look in the mirror and say these words: I forgive you.

Practicing self-forgiveness feels odd, incredibly self-centred and a little bit stupid. But by trying, there is only one thing we have to lose: pain.

I don't know if we can change the world by forgiving ourselves. But we have all seen what happens to people who hold onto their pain. We have watched souls corrode. We have seen what happens to people who believe they don't deserve happiness.

But how can we reach our potential for peace and prosperity, if we continue to live in anger and vengeance? Let's not forget that in the last decade we have also seen forgiveness become a possibility in South Africa, Ireland, Germany, and Canada.

Your heart is the world's heart. Do you think the world can change if our hearts do?

Snow Falling on Valley

"Hello darkness, my old friend/I've come to talk with you again."
— SIMON AND GARFUNKEL

There is a holiness to silence. When you're a kid and you wake up to a hushed sound, you know without thinking that it is snowing. Snow is something of a miracle. Everything looks so different, but for me, it's all about the sound.

The sound of silence.

Woman's Studies scholar Ann McKinnon tells me that sound is different than visual stimuli – sound goes right into the body. Ask any film composer or music producer and they will tell you how sound equals emotion. A song can make tears flow. A few notes can create fear, anticipation, romance – the ears know before the eyes. The space between notes, the backdrop of emotion, is silence. Silence – empty, cavernous, sweet, frightening – our aural reactions speak to us in ways beyond our awareness.

I know people who cannot bear much silence. Whenever I am in a hotel room, I flick on the TV before unpacking; the sound is my companion. The constant hum of a TV or radio tells us we are not alone. Many people cannot live without the sounds of their iPods, stereos, and satellite radios.

What is it about silence that we must avoid?

In many cultures, silence is embraced. Silence helps form the ritual of shared reverence. Anthropologist Rick Goulden states that elders among aboriginal cultures are greeted by the respectful and meaningful use of silence.

"Pausing before speaking, remaining silent after an elder speaks," says Goulden, "demonstrates that you are digesting their words and showing respect for their ideas and knowledge."

When sitting in silence, I think about things that perhaps I don't want to think about. My friend Marie Weale expresses a longing for lost family members that she didn't fully realize until she faced silence.

"Ironically, it was while being alone and sitting in silence that I learned the most about myself."

What happens when we listen to the silence? Certainly, there is no such thing as complete and utter silence. Feet shuffling, coughing, stirring, phone beeping, mind turning – we are never without a soundtrack of constant stimuli.

Greg Krasichynsky states that any "dead air creates a vacuum that must be immediately filled with some sort of information."

He asks a profound question: is silence becoming extinct within our culture?

Writer Joanna Cockerline tells me that "there are so many different silences ... they extend from blissful to agonizing."

Donna Duke says that she's "very comfortable with silence but I live alone and so am used to it and need solitude."

For me, silence is a metaphor for the quiet mind. My mind is constantly turning. It seems there is always something going on in there. Artist Cherie Hanson refers to it as the "hamster wheel," the mind running faster and faster until, in Cherie's words, it runs into itself.

Been there. Done that.

The still mind, the quiet mind, the unoccupied mind, the empty mind – what is there to be gained in reaching such a state? Yoga teacher Jeff Tomlinson calls this quiet state "the space where the mind wants nothing."

Wanting nothing is an idea we see expressed in many religions. It is strongly associated with patience in Christianity and with freedom from desire in Buddhism. Silence here becomes associated with spirituality.

So what does "the extinction of silence" say about the state of spirituality in our world?

I don't know. I do know that bestsellers like "The Shack" and "A New Earth" tell us something about our appetite for spiritual insight if not spiritual awakening.

Eckhart Tolle tells us that "our innermost sense of self, of who you are, is inseparable from stillness. The equivalent of external noise is the inner noise of thinking. The equivalent of external silence is inner stillness."

When Tolle says that true intelligence operates silently, I am reminded of how difficult it is for my mind to find stillness. But apparently this is okay. Life oscillates, so does our attention, so does our consciousness. So being aware of my mind is part of the answer, so say those who know more about these things than I.

No matter what tradition of thinking forms your history, silence is an opportunity to observe – yourself. Just look and just listen. What do you hear?

But what do you do if you are afraid of silence?

"Hello darkness, my old friend," the famous song goes. "I've come to talk with you again." Marshall McLuhan tells us that "darkness is to space what silence is to sound."

In darkness, there is a kind of refuge from things that you can see to things you can't. In acoustic space, there is also a kind of refuge from the eyes, an escape from the dominance of seeing itself, but I will not lie to you: the anxiety remains.

I sometimes lie in bed at night thinking. My mind wanders and I find myself not thinking anymore but listening. I listen to the wind blowing leaves past my window. I listen to the house creak, the furnace vibrate, and the sound of the universe which kind of sounds like a rocky beach with twisted wind-shaped trees and a sliver of moon.

I listen and pretty soon I am listening to myself breathe. I am listening to the blood flowing in my body. I find myself listening to myself listening and then my thoughts leave me altogether and I am listening to something new, something that sounds remarkably like a snowflake fluttering in the black sky toward the ground.

What is the sound that a snowflake makes when spinning against the dark sky? What is the sound of being alive?

I am.

You are.

I am.

You are.

We are.

The Starlight Drive-In

You know me. I'm the little doll that takes your order. I don't need a pen because I know your kind. Chicken chow mein, beef chop suey, honey garlic pork (and lemon chicken on Sundays). I know you. I can smell the scalloped potatoes in your future.

My past is a wonton, and yours is a perogy. I say big diff. You are rude anyway.

Curtis was different. When he came in for the first time, he walked right up to me while I was taking an order from the winners of the Pierre Berton and Anne Murray look-alike contest.

"What do you want?"

"Hi," he said looking at the floor. "I wanted to see if you were okay after what we seen yesterday." He spoke softly. I notice the pearl snap buttons on his checkered cowboy shirt again. I will always like snap buttons now.

"I'm fine," I said. For some reason I wanted to cry. My eyes filled. I felt shaky. He moved quickly and grabbed my arm.

"So, what grade are you in?"

"Seven."

"I'm starved," he said as he pulled me away from the booth and sat me down. He passed me a napkin for my tears and laughed nervously. "You got any kung fu food here or what?"

"Do you want a menu?" I said, dabbing my eyes. The snowbirds left their booth and walked out.

"Get me something good okay? Get me something different. I want what you'd have."

I want what you'd have. I like it when boys say stuff like that.
So I brought him a Coke and a BLT.

"What's a really rude thing people do in here without knowing it?" Curtis asked.

"They put soy sauce on their rice."

"Is that bad? Yikes, don't tell my mom."

"Really bad."

"How come?"

"Soy sauce is for cooking."

"You mean you eat rice like plain?"

"Yeah. Mostly."

"What do you mean mostly?"

"A little Heinz on some fried rice is allowed."

"Who makes these rules?"

"Bruce Lee."

"Fair enough."

"What's something rude I could do at your dinner table?"

"Let me see ..." Curtis put his arms on the table, and leaned his chin in the crook of his elbow. "You know what?"

"What?"

"You can do most anything at an Indian dinner table. You can smoke. You can fart. You can even be a year or two late. The food would be cold though. The one thing you can't do is not put soy sauce on your rice while dressed up as the Lone Ranger."

"The Lone Ranger uses a lot of soy sauce, eh? What about Tonto?"

"Tonto loves Chinese food. Ever been to the Totem Restaurant up in Hazelton?"

"No."

"An Indian runs it."

"Really. How's the food?"

"Bad, but we go anyway."

"How come?"

"'Cause we're all addicted to soy sauce."

Later I slipped him a copy of *Teenbeat* with my name and phone number written on Shaun Cassidy's face.

Sophie Yee. 392-3883. Between 8-9 p.m.

He smiled when he saw my scribbling, and I felt all funny inside.

We met a few days ago in front of our restaurant. A school bus had run over a kid. This kid was an okay kid. When he came to town, the other kids finally had someone weirder than me to tease. What a relief. I felt stupid when they played keep away with the small cloth thing on his head.

Anyways, it took the fire department two hours to flush the streets. He was riding his bike and must've fallen under the wheels. I guess a tire crushed his head. It was so messy. We noticed each other standing there, our faces kind of blank. Curtis came over to me and put a hand on my shoulder. I saw the tears running down his brown cheeks. And now he had come to find me.

To find me.

Nobody had ever looked for me before.

* * *

It's getting late. You think it strange that my sister and I spread our books out on the counter to study? Don't worry. It's all show. Jean lets me talk on the phone because I know her secrets. She got a B in physics and changed it to a B+ with Dad's typewriter. Then she photocopied it and gave it to him. With a B+ she doesn't have to do summer school. Grade twelve will be hard, she says. One mistake and you're working at the Dairy Queen for life.

"How's Injun Joe?" she asks.

"How's your big fat B in physics?" I reply. "The fuzz get you yet?"

"Turn out the lights! It's Mister Stiff Jeans. He's here again!" Jean cries.

Brrrrrrrrrring!

The telephone jangles my nerves. Mister Stiff Jeans starts using the front door for a drum. He's been coming around for a month. Pockmarked cheeks. Crooked dazed eyes. Stooped over like an old man. He's wearing dirty jeans and a logger's wool jacket. He holds out his hand and brings it to his mouth. I pick up the phone before my parents can hear it ring again.

"Hello?"

"Is that you, Sophie?"

"Just a second, okay?" I say gesturing violently to my sister.

"What are you doing?" Curtis asks.

"Nothing," I say urging Jean with my eyes to do something about Mister Stiff Jeans. The man keeps knocking. "Just a sec, Curtis."

"I am not moving," says Jean. I let the phone hang by the cord. It bounces like a Slinky on the floor. I run and open the fridge and pull out a red apple. I shine it on my sleeve. You know this is why mom buys apples. Every day people come and beg us for food. Vitamin C is better than food, Sophie-ya. Jean finally gets up and unlocks the door. I stick my arm out. He takes it. Jean practically slams the door on my arm. He stumbles away holding the apple up to the streetlight.

"Does Injun Joe have any salmon for sale?" Jean smirks.

"Be quiet," I shriek.

"Hi," I say into the phone. I'm out of breath. I'm tense and excited and scared.

"What're you doing?"

"Nothing." I hear a dog barking on his side of the line. And then I hear horns honking.

"Hi," he says, like he's known me my whole life.

"Hi," I whisper nervously. My palms are sweating.

"Ask your sister if she wants coho or sockeye."

"Sorry you heard that."

"I don't mind. I just like to hear your voice," Curtis says. His voice is like suede.

"You like my voice?" I say hopefully.

"It reminds me of someone."

"Who?"

"You."

"Really," I say laughing. Jean leaves and turns off the light.

"Good thing you're you. Otherwise I'd be talking to some stranger that I really like. And I don't want to talk to no stranger."

"Where are you? I hear noises."

"I'm in half a phone booth at the drive-in."

"What's playing?" I say, astonished.

"20,000 Leagues Under the Sea. It's pretty good. But there ain't no Indians in it."

"Any Chinese?"

"Nope," he says. "And I was looking. Jesus Murphy, it's starting to rain."

"You want to go back to the movie?" I imagine him getting cold and shivering.

"No. I like it better this way."

"How come?"

"'Cause they're underwater right now. It's way more realistic when it's raining. Well, so, how about I phone you again tomorrow?"

"I don't think they'll be showing anything good will they?"

"No, they gotta good movie showing then, Sophie."

"Yeah? What's it called?"

"Sophie and Curtis," he says softly.

"Yeah?" I say, weakly.

"You seen it?"

"Is it any good?"

"It's better than 20,000 Leagues. Even when your hair's all wet."

"How does it end?

"You know what, Sophie?

"What?"

"I have three white guys lined up who want to use the phone."

"You gotta go?" I ask worried. "Just hang up, Curtis. Don't get into any trouble."

"What are you talking about?" Curtis asks.

"You said there are three white guys outside the phone booth."

"Yeah?"

"I don't understand."

"That's how the story's going to end."

"The story of us?" I ask.

"Yeah, it's gonna end with three white guys lining up to use the phone."

"You kill me," I say, but really I want to say I really like you or something equally unlike me. I want to say it so bad. I can hear it in my head. I don't even know this boy.

I hear shouting. Some woman is asking Curtis for the telephone.

"The Starlight is a pretty good place to talk to you, except they don't let you use the phone for very long. Bye."

"Bye."

"Bye."

"Bye."

"Double bye."

"Triple bye."

"... You hang up."

"... No, you."

"... I can't."

"... Me neither."

"Bye, honey!" a woman shouts in my ear. Then I hear silence.

The fridge motor goes off and shudders. A logging truck rumbles by. My left ear is still hot. It rains diagonally. Two days ago, I saw a kid's brains on the pavement. Yesterday, an Indian boy walks into my restaurant because he's looking for me. Tonight, he calls me from the Starlight with his hair soaked.

I am thirteen years old, I say to myself. I am thirteen years old. This is what it feels like to be alive. Never forget this feeling. Never.

It's been a lifetime since I talked to him. Okay, probably two weeks.

The last time he called, we had our first and last fight.

"You ever get bugged about being a Chinaman, Sophie? He asked.

"Yeah." I replied. Already I felt uneasy. He liked to talk about this stuff.

"Why do they call us Indians?" he asked. "They're from India. They're the goddamn real Indians. No wonder he got squashed. You didn't push him under that bus did you?"

"Screw you!" I screamed. And then we listened to each other breathe for a while.

"I noticed you," he said softly. "Because you were the only one who looked sad."

"I don't want to be noticed," I said angrily. "Ever again."

"Bye, then," he whispered.

"Bye," I said feeling stupid and scared that my life was blowing away. Two byes and then he was gone. Jesus Murphy. Two byes are barely the minimum.

* * *

It is the last lunch hour sock hop of grade seven. The gym floor shines in the low light. The boys line up on one side. We're on the other. All of us in our sock feet mop up the dust on the floor. Some of the grade six boys pretend to curl in their wool socks. My father doesn't understand the sport of curling. Nobody oriental does. Two boys from my grade play ruler hockey with a rolled up sock. My father loves hockey. He falls asleep as soon as he hears the theme from Hockey Night in Canada. I love Borje Salming.

Smoking in the boy's room. Smoking in the boy's room.

I don't care to hear this song again.

Some of the boys have holes in their socks. Their big obscene toes shine like only big obscene toes can. The boys can't stop from asking me to dance. I cannot dance with a boy who has his toenails showing.

Really, it's just not me.

On girl's choice, I dance with my friend Antonia. She has breasts galore and gets attention from everybody. Who doesn't know she got her period in grade five? Grade five! She sweats under her arms like the Quebecker guy who washes dishes in our restaurant, and I can smell that weird sour scent when we dance. I don't think I stink at all because I eat french fries and BLTs. Do you know what it's like to have your breasts hurt and feel like infected pimples? I am not memorizing that feeling.

Do you realize that if I ate rice and sweet and sour pork, the garlic would ooze out of me and hang around me like a fog? Just like Mom and Dad on Friday nights when we put on the smorgasbord. Their skin is oily like mine. What a curse. To have your pores fertilized by an oily forehead. Thank god for the straight black bangs.

Stop squeezing them, Sophie. And stop smelling everything.

This sock hop won't be one to remember. I go because my friends say we are going. I go because it's raining outside and what else is there to do? Not all the girls have boys asking them. I don't want anybody to ask me. I don't want some earnest boy talking to my chest or punching my shoulder. I have pretty much forgotten about Curtis now.

This dance is dumb. We all say that. But we all go anyway. It is getting hot inside, so the teachers throw open the exit doors.

Exit

Exit

Exit

I love the soft red glow of the exit signs. Soon it will be the last dance, and I will return with my shoes to the security of my desk and the light of day. Then I see his silhouette at the side door. The teachers are outside smoking. He takes off his boots and moves toward me. He tosses his jean jacket on the floor.

"Can I have this dance?" Curtis asks, taking my hand. I know the other girls are looking at him. And at me. Curtis is in grade nine.

We are in grade seven. He is so tall. He might as well be – he might as well be a man.

And what about me? What am I?

Out on the gym floor, he grabs my belt loops as the song begins. It is my favourite, the one by Edward Bear. He pulls me toward him. I listen to the lyrics that I will remember all my life.

"It's the last song I'll ever write for you. It's the last time that I'll tell you just how much I really care."

He holds me in his arms, and I can feel the pearl snap buttons against me. I close my eyes, and I feel powerful like I am growing into someone. He smells like suede and cigarettes and cinnamon, like the inside of my mom's purse. I hold my arms around his neck.

Do you know how it is to slip away, to feel yourself disappearing and then reappearing as someone else? It is time, I think, to memorize this feeling.

Screw that.

I am too busy dancing.

He's a boy off the reserve and I am a cook's girl. I imagine the stars spinning around the sky. The soundtrack swells. We are dancing on the roof of the Starlight Drive-In. There is a romantic movie playing in the distance. Three white guys wait for the pay phone.

Some Things Never Change

30 YEAR HIGH SCHOOL REUNION

Across the street from the Burnaby North Senior Secondary sits an Italian restaurant with an outdoor patio and six statues of half-naked people. I pulled my car into a fenced parking lot that used to be a drive-in restaurant.

I used to eat free Teen burgers there because, well, I was a teen and because I knew the Korean owners, the Kangs. You could barely make out where the building used to be, like chalk lines at a crime scene.

It was sprinkling in a classic Vancouver-style mist. Some things never change.

Inside the restaurant, I received a nametag and two drink tickets. The nametag had my high school photo on it. I stuck it on my chest and did what I usually do when I face socially awkward situations: I headed for the bar.

I checked my watch. It was 7 p.m. I don't recognize anybody except for Van Beek, who organized our thirtieth high school reun-ion using Facebook.

"Glad you could make it," Van Beek said with a smile. "Styan and I wondered if you would come."

Van Beek, Styan, Yip, Ronning, and Deschner (of the Okanagan) – these were the popular jocks of Burnaby North. They were cool and popular.

Chung, Wong, Chow, Mao – we were the Asian academic

crowd, complete with calculators, buckteeth, and ill-fitting pants — and that was just me.

"I'm here," I said to Van Beek, shaking his hand. I took a sip of red wine and looked at the door. Would DiTosto show up?

DiTosto used to trip me on the way to class. He shoved me into lockers. To say he was a racist wouldn't be quite accurate. He was a racist and a bully. If you were East Indian, like my friend Gadhia, you had it even worse.

After a few long minutes of standing in the corner with my pal, Wong, who made me attend this function, I started questioning my memory. Did I really attend high school with all these people? Why couldn't I recognize anyone?

I headed for some comfort. I walked toward two guys who also stood on the outskirts of the bar.

"Hello," I said. "Is this the Asian section?"

"Yeah," Okano said. "We look damn good. You actually recognized us, didn't you?"

"Yeah," Cruz said, "'cause some things never change."

We stood there laughing. Me, a Korean guy who didn't want to be there. Okano, a lanky Japanese guy. And Cruz, a Filipino brother from Rutland.

Over in the corner is my pal Wong. He's actually Canadian born Chinese. His grandparents worked in the Cumberland coalmines and did the laundry for rich Vancouver families. Beside him is RWong; he's from Malaysia and speaks with a Kiwi accent. All five of us look like we could play on one team, but we share nothing except a look and the safety in numbers concept.

More people trickled into the restaurant until there were about 80 of us. After a few more drinks, I was done with being shy. I walked to one of the most beautiful women in grade twelve, a stunning woman who still looked like one of the Charlie's Angels.

"Hello, Linda," I said with the élan of the Okanagan College Dean of Arts and Foundational Programs, do you remember me?"

"What?" she said.

"Remember ME?"

"No."

This is the great thing about high school reunions. You get to meet new people.

Outside where the smokers are, I catch up to Van Beek and Styan. In high school we shared a friend, Yip, a Chinese brother who drove a Camaro and hung with the popular crowd. In university he abandoned his old high school friends and started hanging around with me.

"You need me to help you with your calculus or something?" I remembered asking him.

Styan smiled. He was one of the rare students who could talk to the jocks, slum with the musicians, hang with us coloured folk, and still retain a suave coolness. Styan, after thirty years, hadn't changed much.

"Glad you could make it," Styan said. "I know high school was tough on you, but I respected you guys."

"High school was great," a grad with blonde hair and a nice neckline interrupted. "It was the greatest time of my life."

"It was the worst for me," I said.

"How could it be?" She asked nearly offended. When I explained, she shook her head.

"No. That's not the way it was. Was it?"

Then Styan stepped in.

"It's all true," he said. "You don't remember DiTosto?"

"DiTosto?" She said.

"Yeah," Styan said. "He was bad."

Then I talked to Bedford, Yue, and Hester and I couldn't believe what Bedford was talking about: polyamory legal defenses. I talked to Manifold and Woolverton and I couldn't believe what was actually happening to me.

I started seeing high school in a different way, a better way, maybe a less true way, but a more forgiving way.

Here we all were in this loud and crowded restaurant on East

Hastings with so much more in common than differences. We were middle-class kids who dreamed of nothing more than getting a job, raising a family, and having a little security.

Many of my classmates, like the gorgeous Manifold, had gone overseas, searched out her dreams and returned home so that her kids could live safe and happy lives.

When talking about my wife and children, I realized that we were all here for the same reasons. We weren't there to discuss what was essentially a racially-segregated high school, or talk about what was in our garages; we were there to share a life experience.

We talked about teachers quite a bit. Remember Mr. Wilson? Remember Mr. Meyer. Remember him? Remember her?

Remember how good it is to remember?

I met people at my high school reunion that I have never seen before. I met them and we laughed and we talked about some very serious things: race, class, gender, marriage, childhood, and parents.

We didn't talk about money or job titles. Our topic seemed to be about searching and accepting. Accepting for our true selves, searching for meaning, accepting what love came our way.

We also talked about gratitude. We knew there were people who couldn't be there. High school was high school, but maybe things weren't so great now. I may have been teased, but many had a rougher road than me.

Kirkwood, Ogasawara, Pardely, Perry, Sillars – I didn't think I'd be so darned grateful to see you.

At about midnight, it was getting drunky and huggy, so I decided to split. The elegant Van Beek shook my hand at the door. An old buddy, Pich, slapped me on the back and said he was really glad to see me.

"Stan, buddy!"

I confess I almost cried when I saw him. Do you know how it feels to see someone who remembers you so fondly?

Pich was on his own now. He had a boy he adored, and even had a girlfriend in Kelowna.

"Dude," I said. "Next time you're town, you don't buy drinks; I do."

As I left the restaurant, I wasn't thinking anymore about past wounds.

I started thinking about how beautiful it was to remember old friendships, and how much more beautiful it was to forgive and try for something more.

Burnaby has changed so much, I thought, as I walked to the parking lot. It was still drizzling. I could barely make out my high school standing in the distance. I looked up at the night sky and felt the rain on my face and laughed.

ACKNOWLEDGEMENTS

It takes a lifetime to write a book like this. I want to name everyone who has either kissed or kicked me. You need both to get very far.

Gratitude goes to the former editors of the *Kelowna Daily Courier*, Tom Wilson, for commissioning the column, Global Citizen, in 2006. Tom nurtured the work. Jon Manchester, a former managing editor, has been a stalwart editor and supporter.

This work owes its evolution to the readers of *The Okanagan Sunday*. Your comments and feedback raised the work and pushed me into challenging territory. I am so grateful for the emails I received from readers on those Sunday mornings when I wondered what I had written. Thank you Jim Taylor, Darren Handschuh, and Ross Freake.

Supporters of my development include people like Henry Kim, Veronica Gaylie, Jill Garrett, John Lent, Rob Crobar, and Daniel Miller, whom I counted on as readers and fellow writers. Tim Jacobs, this work would not be without you.

Thanks to loyal readers Karla Chase, Richard Chung, Joanna Cockerline, Cherie Hansen, Howard Hisdal, Bob Holtby, Gloria Huang-Storie, Ana Lopez, Ann McKinnon, Naheed Nenshi, Anna Romano, Keith Shanks, Stuart Storie, Peter Urmetzer, and Davidicus Wong.

I offer much appreciation to my friends and colleagues at Okanagan College and Camosun College.

Robert Huxtable supported these pages. Dale Mosher and Seana Dombrosky proofread them. Robert Belton nurtured them. The late Reverend Albert Baldeo gave them confidence.

I want to thank the people who exist inside these pages: Ji Wong Chung, Sook Ja Chung, Heidi MacPherson, Frank Trenouth, Andy Gibbs, Sherrin Western, Brent MacDonald, Piet Kamstra, Bob MacPherson, Kayo Kamstra, Bong Choon Chung, and Kevin Ferris.

Thank you to my ancestors past and future.

With or without this work, it is Alberta Kamstra who inspires me. Alberta, everything I do, I do to honour and respect our love. Our children, Beckett and Clementine, will always be our greatest achievement.

Alberta, Beckett, and Clementine, I dedicate this book to you.

ABOUT THE AUTHOR

Stan Chung is an award-winning writer, and, at the time of this writing, was the Dean of Arts and Sciences at Camosun College. He is currently Vice President Academic and Applied Research at the College of the Rockies.

He was born in Seoul, raised in Williams Lake, and studied at UBC (BA Hons), University of Toronto (MA), Simon Fraser University (PDP) and UBC (PhD).

Stan is well-known for his ability to provide visionary, consultative, and transformative leadership. His 22 years of experience in the BC college sector includes six years of senior experience as Director, Associate Dean, Acting Dean and Dean. In 2008 he was selected as one of 230 to attend the Governor General's Canadian Leadership Conference.

A passionate advocate for innovation and learning, he speaks regularly on educational issues while pursuing scholarly interests in transformational learning, community leadership, and advocacy journalism.

Stan maintains an active community profile as a writer with over 600 published articles in a variety of publications. He was runner-up at the CBC Literary Awards and has published in *AdBusters, Mission Review, Kelowna Daily Courier, Pentiction Herald,* and *Prince George Citizen.* His feature column Global Citizen is pub-lished in *The Okanagan Sunday.*

Stan is married with two children. He spends his time between West Kelowna and Cranbrook, BC.

Books Stan Chung:
Global Citizen: River of Love and other essays
I Held My Breath for a Year: and other essays

Books can per purchased at Amazon
in paperback and eBook format

Team Published with assistance from
Artistic Warrior Publishing
www.artisticwarrior.com

For more information visit stanchung.ca

Thank you for supporting a Canadian Author

www.ingramcontent.com/pod-product-compliance
Lightning Source LLC
Chambersburg PA
CBHW050127030726
47505CB00007B/2070